William Peterfield Trent

English Culture in Virginia

A Study of the Gilmer Letters and an Account of the English Professors Obtained by

Jefferson for the University of Virginia

William Peterfield Trent

English Culture in Virginia
A Study of the Gilmer Letters and an Account of the English Professors Obtained by Jefferson for the University of Virginia

ISBN/EAN: 9783337817435

Printed in Europe, USA, Canada, Australia, Japan

Cover: Foto ©Thomas Meinert / pixelio.de

More available books at **www.hansebooks.com**

V-VI

English Culture in Virginia

JOHNS HOPKINS UNIVERSITY STUDIES

IN

HISTORICAL AND POLITICAL SCIENCE

HERBERT 'B. ADAMS, Editor

History is past Politics and Politics present History—*Freeman*

SEVENTH SERIES

V-VI

English Culture in Virginia

A STUDY OF THE GILMER LETTERS AND AN ACCOUNT OF THE
ENGLISH PROFESSORS OBTAINED BY JEFFERSON
FOR THE UNIVERSITY OF VIRGINIA

BY WILLIAM P. TRENT, M. A.

Professor of History in the University of the South

BALTIMORE

N. MURRAY, PUBLICATION AGENT, JOHNS HOPKINS UNIVERSITY

May and June, 1889

TABLE OF CONTENTS.

INTRODUCTION.

About a year ago the Editor of these Studies honored me by desiring my coöperation in the work he had undertaken with regard to the history of education in Virginia. ·I accordingly furnished two chapters for his monograph on "Thomas Jefferson and the University of Virginia," published by the United States Bureau of Education, Circular of Information, No. 1, 1888. But one seldom begins a line of investigation without being led to deeper research than he had at first intended; and so it was in the present case.

This new and independent study has been mainly developed from the correspondence of Francis Walker Gilmer. Who Mr. Gilmer was and what he did—things worth knowing but known to very few—will appear fully hereafter, for even the author of a "study" may occasionally borrow a device from the novelist and keep his readers in suspense; but it will be necessary to explain at the outset how the aforesaid correspondence came into my hands. The facts of the case are briefly these. Dr. Adams was informed by a gentlemen whom he had consulted about the work previously mentioned, that a volume of letters relating to the early history of the University of Virginia was in the hands of John Gilmer, Esquire, of Chatham, Virginia. A letter to that gentleman brought a courteous reply and the desired volume. Being much pressed by his professional and other duties, Dr. Adams handed me this voluminous correspondence with the request that I would examine it and express an opinion as to its value with regard to that period of the University's history on which he was specially engaged. I did examine it with great care, and found that, although it did not bear directly on the field of investigation Dr. Adams had chosen, it nevertheless

7

opened up a new field of hardly inferior interest.   Upon this
report Dr. Adams and Mr. Gilmer were kind enough to intrust
the letters to me that I might complete a study, the outlines of
which were already developing themselves in my own mind.   In
a letter to my mother I alluded to the fact that this task had
been confided to me.   She at once wrote me that she was certain
another volume of a similar character was in existence, and that
she would endeavor to obtain it for me.

Her statement proved true and the companion volume is now
in my hands through the kindness of Mrs. Emma Breckinridge,
of "Grove Hill," Botetourt County, Virginia.   Mrs. Breckinridge is a sister of Mr. John Gilmer and a daughter of Peachy
Gilmer, the eldest brother of the subject of this sketch.   This
second volume is even more invaluable than the first as it contains all of Gilmer's own letters to Mr. Jefferson, &c., and also
throws many valuable side lights upon the internal history of
Virginia for the period from 1815 to 1825.   How and why these
letters, nearly 700 in number, were bound and preserved will
appear in the sequel.   It will be sufficient here to ask indulgence
for the mistakes which have doubtless crept into my work, and
to return my hearty thanks to the friends who have assisted me
in an investigation not wanting in complexity and minute details.

WILLIAM P. TRENT.

The University of the South,
    December 1, 1888.

ENGLISH CULTURE IN VIRGINIA.

CHAPTER I.

THE DEVELOPMENT OF THE UNIVERSITY IDEA.

At the beginning of this century what culture Virginia had was not Virginian. This is not a Virginia bull, but a deplorable fact. There was no lack of great men or of highly cultivated men. A Virginian occupied the Presidential chair, and three others had it in reversion. Patrick Henry was dead, but John Randolph, by his eloquence and wit and sarcasm, was making Congress doubt whether it loved him or hated him. At the Richmond bar were Marshall and Wickham and Wirt, while at Norfolk men were beginning to prophesy great things of an eloquent young lawyer,—Littleton Waller Tazewell. There were hundreds of well educated men riding over their plantations or congregating on court day either to hear or to make speeches—and even the bar of as small a place as Winchester could boast of speakers whom these educated men would willingly hear. Although there was a servile, ignorant mass beneath them, this could not then be helped, nor had the habits of inaction, thereby necessarily engendered, extended as fully as they afterwards did, to the affairs of mind. Travel was not uncommon. One old gentleman was "gigomaniac" enough to drive to Boston in his gig every other summer, the return visit of his New England friends being made, it is supposed, during the summers his gig was mending. Although Mr. Jefferson and his colleagues had swept away every vestige they could of the feudal system, primogeniture in education was an every day fact—unjust as primogeniture generally is, but still a bright spot in the history of education in Virginia. Not a few families managed to send one representative at least to Europe for study and travel, and that representative was usually the eldest son. If England seemed too far, one or more of the sons went to Princeton or to William and Mary—many shutting their eyes to the fact that the latter historic place was even then slowly dying. Edinburgh, of course, was the goal of a young medical student's desires; but if he could not "compass this golden hope," Philadelphia was willing to receive him hospitably and to give him the benefit of her lectures and museums for a good round price. Books and libraries were not abundant; but the books were at least good, however exorbitant their cost—a serious item in the culture of a state fast ruining itself financially by an extravagant hospitality.

In some families it had been a custom to direct the factor in London to send back with the proceeds of the tobacco, a pipe of Madeira and a fixed amount of current literature— and hence it is that one occasionally comes across a rare first edition when rummaging the library of an old country house. Now if a boy had a taste for reading, he needed not to grow up an ignoramus even if he were not sent to college; but if he preferred his gun and horse, there were few to thwart him, his father having to look after the estate, tutors and schoolmasters being *rarae aves,* and the mother having enough on her hands in the housekeeping and the bringing up of her daughters, who, though they knew nothing of moral philossophy and aesthetics, had, nevertheless read Pope and the Spectator, and kept in their memories household receipts of considerable claim to genealogical pride.

But I said that the culture in Virginia was not Virginian, and I have not sufficiently explained my meaning. I do not mean to imply the same reproach as is implied in the hackneyed invocation for " the great American novel." The culture in Virginia was naturally English modified by circumstances peculiar to a slaveholding, sparsely settled society. It was modified, too, by the birth of the feeling of independence and by the desire to try wings not fully fledged. All this was natural and is certainly not reprehensible. But there is another sense in which culture in Virginia was not Virginian, which if it does not imply reproach, must certainly cause a feeling of regret even to us of this late day. I.refer to the almost universal lack of any primary and secondary instruction worthy of the name, and to the comparative lack of university instruction. William and Mary College had for many years done a great work in Virginia, but though buoyed up for a time by the wisdom of Mr. Jefferson as a visitor, and of Bishop Madison as president, its influence was fast waning and, before the first quarter of the century had gone by, was practically null. Hampden Sidney seems to have been little more than a high-school, and it has at all times been sectarian. Washington College (since Washington and Lee University) did not exert a large influence,[1] and hence it was that Princeton drew away sons from nearly every Virginia family of importance. When the foundation of a state university was being urged upon the legislature, a prominent Presbyterian clergyman of Richmond, Dr. Rice, made a calculation and found that over $250,000 were annually sent out of Virginia to support youths at the various foreign schools and colleges. This does not look as if many Virginians patronized the three institutions above mentioned ; but at any rate, it shows that a university of high grade was one of the needs of the people.[2]

---

[1] In one of the early volumes of Dr. Rice's " Virginia Evangelical and Literary Magazine " (I think the sixth) a short account of the studies pursued at this college and a list of the instructors will be found. From this the truth of the above statement will be apparent.

[2] See Dr. Adams' " Jefferson and the Univ. of Va.," p. 98.

With regard to secondary and primary instruction the out-
look was decidedly worse. Towns like Richmond had, of
course, fair schools; but the country districts were almost
entirely unprovided with even the rudest village schools.
From a letter of John Taylor of Caroline, found among the
Gilmer papers, I learned that there was a fairly prosperous
boarding school in that county in 1817—but this was the
exception, not the rule. It is true that just before the beginning of the century the legislature had passed a law with
regard to the establishment of primary schools; but this law
had been a dead letter because it was left to the county judges
to decide whether such schools were necessary or not, and
because the judges were, as might have been expected, either
too conservative or too lazy to attend to such an innovation
or such a small matter as a primary school. Education in
Virginia, then, may be said to have been at a stand still, or
rather on the decline, when Mr. Jefferson gave up his federal
honors and betook himself to Monticello.[1]

The short annals of our country, however little they are
attended to, are even in times of peace by no means destitute
of "moving incidents;" and, though for the reader's sake
I forbear the usual quotation from Milton, I cannot refrain
from dwelling upon one of them. Although one may doubt
whether Jefferson's mind was of the highest order, it can
hardly be denied that he has impressed his personality and
his doctrines more strongly upon posterity than has any
other American. Although his brilliant rival's influence is
still to be felt in our federal finances, and although Andrew
Jackson is the representative of many distinctively American
political ideas, it would still seem that a larger number of
our countrymen look to Jefferson as the leader of their November choral song than to any other of our statesmen, living

---

[1] The laudable efforts of the Scotch Irish settlers to provide education for
their families ought not to be overlooked; but these men were poor and
unable to accomplish great things.

or dead—and I know not of a better test of creative genius in politics. It was this man who left the sphere of national affairs to impress himself upon Virginia education; and I cannot but contradict myself and say that his victory should be " no less renowned."

It is a glorious picture—to see a man who has tasted the sweetness of power, a man who could reasonably look forward to the ease and comfort of a dignified retirement, a man who, if he must work, might at least turn his talents to account in building up a fortune already shattered by an extravagant generosity, becoming the foremost in a movement, properly devolving on younger men, an arduous task well nigh impossible of success—the task of raising Virginia from the slough of ignorance and inaction. This he accomplished, and although it seems necessary for the authorities of the University of Virginia to state in their annual announcements that their institution was founded by Thomas Jefferson, there are a few men living who know the last work of the old patriot was as great and glorious as any of the successes of his vigorous manhood.[1] A short sketch of this work seems necessary as an introduction to the task I have undertaken of giving to the world some account of the labors

---

[1] This cannot be said of his latest biographer, Mr. John T. Morse, Jr., who devotes only thirteen very general lines to what Mr. Jefferson deemed worthy to form one of the three services to his country for which posterity were to thank him when looking upon his tomb. Even a professedly political biography should have said more than this, for assuredly a statesman's attitude toward popular education must count for much when we come to estimate his statesmanship. Mr. James Parton devoted over eight pages to the subject and was thoughtful and painstaking enough to write to the chairman of the faculty (Col. C. S. Venable) for information about the University. In this connection it may not be amiss to quote Mr. Madison. "The University of Virginia, as a temple dedicated to science and liberty, was, after his retirement from the political sphere, the object nearest his heart and so continued to the close of his life. His devotion to it was intense and his exertions untiring. It bears the stamp of his genius and will be a noble monument of his fame." Madison's Writings, Cong. Ed. 1865, III, 533.

of one who was not the least of Mr. Jefferson's coadjutors in
this work of Virginia's redemption.

About the year 1814 certain monies found themselves in
the hands of the trustees of an institution still in embryo—
the Albemarle Academy. These trustees were the leading
men of the county and among them Mr. Jefferson towered—
physically as well as intellectually. How to spend the money
most profitably was, of course, the paramount question. In
a letter to his nephew, Peter Carr, one of the trustees, Jefferson sketched a plan of what Virginia education ought to be—
a plan legitimately evolved from his bill of 1779 for the
more general diffusion of knowledge. This letter was published in the Richmond *Enquirer* of September 7, 1814,
and of course attracted great attention not only on account
of the fame of its writer, but also on account of the wisdom
and boldness of the scheme which it proposed. So comprehensive was this scheme that many a conservative head was
shaken, some going so far as to say that the old philosopher
was in his dotage. But no chemist has ever been more
familiar with the properties of common substances, than was
Mr. Jefferson with the characteristics of his fellow citizens.
He knew the pulse of Virginia public opinion to a beat, and
he felt that he would succeed through the very boldness of
his plans. It was easy enough to persuade the trustees of
Albemarle Academy to petition the legislature that a college might be substituted for a school—Central College also
destined to remain in the embryo state. It was not difficult
to obtain the consent of the legislature that Albermarle
Academy should cease to be and Central College begin to
be—for as yet that very sensitive nerve of the body politic,
the financial nerve, had not been bunglingly touched. And
so during the session of 1815–16 Central College in the
County of Albermarle was duly established and given a
board of trustees. Three members of this board have some
claim to remembrance on the part of posterity—they were
Thomas Jefferson, James Madison, and James Monroe. There

were others, too, who shall not go unnoticed. Possibly many
thought that the establishment of this new college near his
favorite town of Charlottesville, which he would fain have
had the capital of the state, would satisfy Mr. Jefferson and
enable him to die in peace. But the shrewd old gentleman
was by no means satisfied; he bided his time, however, for
now he saw light ahead, having a fellow workman whom his
heart loved.

If Mr. Jefferson was the father of the University of Virginia Joseph Carrington Cabell certainly took infinite pains
in teaching the child to walk. Born in 1778 of a distinguished and patriotic father, Colonel Nicholas Cabell, he was
now (1817) in the prime of manhood. After graduating at
William and Mary he had gone to Europe for his health,
and, having recruited that, had studied in more than one
of the leading universities. While in Switzerland, he had
visited and conversed with Pestalozzi, and thus began that
subtle connection of the University of Virginia with great
men, which I hope to bring out strongly in the following
pages. Meeting with President Jefferson on his return to
this country, he began an intimacy which only ceased twenty
years afterward at the death of the venerable statesman—an
intimacy by which Mr. Jefferson was finally enabled to see
his glorious idea realized in very fact.

Declining all offers of diplomatic position under the general government, Mr. Cabell plunged into the politics of his
state, actuated by the idea so prevalent at the time that more
distinction awaited the statesman in this circumscribed sphere
than could possibly be obtained in the larger one of federal
affairs. He was now an influential member of the state senate
when Mr. Jefferson enlisted his aid in behalf of his pet
schemes. That aid was willingly and efficiently vouchsafed,
and has been commemorated by the publication of the Jefferson-Cabell Correspondence, a work containing valuable
information but not so sifted and arranged as to be of much

use to the general reader.[1] The rest of this chapter will,
however, be mainly derived from it.

On July 28, 1817, a called meeting of the trustees of the
Central College was held at Mr. Madison's seat, Montpelier,
in Orange County. There were present Thomas Jefferson,
James Madison, Joseph C. Cabell, and John H. Cocke. The
latter gentleman (1780–1866) was, from the beginning, a great
friend to the university. He had attained some distinction in
the war of 1812 as an efficient general, though inclining to the
martinet. He was also known far and wide for his temper-
ance proclivities. But we have more especially to notice the
first steps taken toward importing culture into Virginia in the
shape of efficient teachers. We find the following record spread
upon the minutes of this meeting:

"It is agreed that application be made to Dr. Knox, of
Baltimore, to accept the Professorship of Languages, Belles-
Lettres, Rhetoric, History and Geography ; and that an independent salary of five hundred dollars, with a perquisite of
twenty-five dollars for each pupil, together with chambers for
his accommodation, be allowed him as a compensation for his
services, he finding the necessary assistant ushers."

If the reader be curious to know what kind of a Doctor this
gentleman was, I take pleasure in informing him that he was
a clergyman, and that, although the *second* man called to a
chair in Mr. Jefferson's college was an undoubted liberal, the
first was highly orthodox. I leave this fact to those who,
after sixty years, have not ceased from the hue and cry raised
when Dr. Cooper was elected a professor in Central College.

But although two deists voted for the Rev. Dr. Knox as
the first professor in their new college, I would not have it
supposed that Mr. Jefferson was not disappointed. The following extract from a letter to Mr. Cabell, of January 5,

---

[1] "Early History of the University of Virginia as contained in the
letters of Thomas Jefferson and Joseph C. Cabell, &c." Richmond, J. W.
Randolph, 1856.

1815, will give the reader some idea of what that disappointment must have been :

"I think I have it now in my power to obtain three of the ablest characters in the world to fill the higher professorships of what in the plan is called the second, or general grade of education; [he refers here to his letter to Peter Carr, which the reader can find in the Jefferson-Cabell correspondence, page 384] three such characters as are not in a single university of Europe; and for those of languages and mathematics, a part of the same grade, able professors doubtless could also be readily obtained. With these characters, I should not be afraid to say that the circle of the sciences composing that second, or general grade, would be more profoundly taught here than in any institution in the United States, and I might go farther."[1] The three characters alluded to were Say, the great economist, who had recently written to Mr. Jefferson, proposing to come and settle near Monticello, a design which he never carried out; Dr. Thomas Cooper, of whom more anon; and possibly, nay probably, the Abbé Corrèa, a profound natural historian then lecturing in Philadelphia, and likely to be often introduced into these pages.[2] What wonder that Mr. Jefferson felt disappointed in having no one to vote for but Dr. Knox, of Baltimore !

The next meeting of the trustees was held at Charlottesville on the 7th of October, 1817, and we find the following entry, which is of importance to us :

---

[1] Jefferson-Cabell Correspondence, p. 37.
[2] Dr. Adams suggests, p. 65, that Destutt Tracy was the third character, because of his attainments as an "ideologist." This is by no means improbable; but Corrèa was omniscient and the date of the above letter tallies so well with his visit to Monticello that I still hold to the above opinion. Besides the whole subject of moral philosophy would thus have been intrusted to a man not identified with our people—a thing which Jefferson was always opposed to. This objection would not have applied to Cooper, who could have taught Ideology, Law, and almost everything else—while Corrèa could have taught the rest ! Besides Say and Tracy would have clashed, both being economists.

" On information that the Rev. Mr. Knox, formerly thought of for a professor of languages, is withdrawn from business, the order of July the 28th is rescinded, and it is resolved to offer, in the first place, the professorship of Chemistry, &c., to Doct. Thomas Cooper of Pennsylvania, adding to it that of law, with a fixed salary of $1,000, and tuition fees of $20 from each of his students, to be paid by them, &c." [1]

Here it seems proper to say a word or two with regard to this remarkable man. Doctor Thomas Cooper was born in London in 1759 and died in Columbia, S. C., in 1840. He practiced law in England, and was one of the representatives sent by the English democratic clubs to France during the Revolution. I find his different vocations summed up in an amusing way by a half mad philosopher and schoolmaster, James Ogilvie, of whom I shall have more to say hereafter. In a letter to Francis Walker Gilmer, Ogilvie says of Cooper: " He has undergone as many metamorphoses as Proteus. Ovid would certainly have immortalized him. In the course of the last twenty years he has been Farmer, Lawyer, Patriot, Judge, Belles-lettres cognoscenti and Professor of Chemistry, to which will shortly be added Doctor in Medicine and Professor of Law. As farmer he spent all his money, as lawyer he made some—as patriot the Federalists imprisoned him—as Judge the Democrats became enraged at him. *Then* the Federalists made him professor of Chemistry, at which he remains — . . . . He became weary of living single and married about twenty months ago, the consequence is he has a young daughter." The best part of this amusing catalogue is that it is every word true. To this list of callings I can add that of calico printing in Manchester, at which he failed, and of statute-revising in South Carolina—at which he died. He came to this country in 1795 and settled with Priestley at Lancaster, Pennsylvania, in which state most of the exploits celebrated by Ogilvie were performed. After being compelled by

---

[1] Jefferson and Cabell Correspondence, p. 397.

the clamor raised about his religious opinions to give up all idea of entering Mr. Jefferson's new institution, he went to South Carolina and became connected with the college at Columbia. He was a truly remarkable man, and published treatises on almost every known subject, beginning with Justinian's Institutes.

But returning from this digression, we find Mr. Jefferson more hopeful, now that it looks as if he were going to get at least one of his three " characters." Why not take advantage of the annual report that must be made by the trustees to the legislature and suggest that instead of Central College (good in itself, but still a mere college) the state herself found an University to be the top stone of a noble edifice to be known to posterity as the Virginia system of education? No sooner had this thought attained to fair proportions in his brain than the thing was done. To influence the other trustees was easy, and, with Cabell and his friends in the legislature, even that august body was brought to look upon the plan with favor, little foreseeing how soon the financial nerve was to be shocked. Accordingly on the sixth day of January in the year 1818, it was proposed that the property of Central College should become a nucleus for funds to be applied to the establishment of a true state university upon a respectable scale.

It would be useless to describe the wagging of conservative beards, more than useless to describe the tortures gone through by timid legislators speculating how their constituents would construe their votes. There was then in existence a Literary Fund, how formed matters not, which Mr. Jefferson's eyes had fastened upon. The financial nerve must be shocked, but delicately, and here was a way to do it. Accordingly an act appropriating part of the revenue of the Literary Fund, &c., passed on the 21st of February, 1818. So far, so good—but an all important question arises. Where shall the new University be? Now the lobbying and wireworking begin. There are several parts of the state which would not

object to becoming the seat of the Muses. Staunton, for
instance, does not see at all why Charlottesville should carry
off the prize. Wherefore a Commission is appointed to sit at
Rockfish Gap, in the Blue Ridge, to determine a site for Virginia's University which all parties are now agreed must be
something good of its kind.

This Commission sat on the first day of August, 1818, and
was largely attended ; the two ex-presidents heading the list
of names.[1] Here Mr. Jefferson produced a map of the state
and showed that Charlottesville was the centre of everything—certainly of his own desires. Who could refuse to
gratify such a man as he stood there crowned with age and
honors, and flushed with enthusiasm for an object both needful and glorious? Sectional jealousies were stifled, and Charlottesville was chosen as the site of the future University.[2]
But the Commission did not dissolve before it had presented
a report as to what ought to be taught in the new institution—a report in which Mr. Jefferson's hand is, of course, to
be seen.[3] They recommended that ten professorships should
be established as follows : (1) Ancient Languages, (2) Modern
Languages, (3) Mathematics, pure, (4) Physico-Mathematics,
(5) Physics or Natural Philosophy, (6) Botany and Zoölogy,
(7) Anatomy and Medicine, (8) Government, Political Economy, &c., (9) Law Municipal, (10) Ideology, Ethics, &c.
This was as comprehensive a scheme as even Mr. Jefferson
could have wished, for did it not include his favorite Anglo-
Saxon under the head of Modern Languages? But further
the Commission advised that buildings be furnished wherein
gymnastics might be taught, but did not advance to the modern

---

[1] It is generally stated that President Monroe attended this meeting.
This I am inclined to doubt, if the list of the signers of the Report be
correct, and I afterwards discovered that Mr. Randall had noted the same
error (Life of Jefferson, III, 463), if error it be.

[2] Jefferson-Cabell Correspondence, page 432.

[3] Jefferson had consulted John Adams as to a scheme of professorships
two years before. Adams' Works, X, 213.

idea (or is it modern?) of having a special professor to teach them.[1]   Thus the Rockfish Gap Commission set in glory.

The legislature receiving its report passed an act on the 25th of January, 1819, establishing the University of Virginia upon pretty much the same plan as that recommended by the Commission, leaving the visitors of Central College to fulfil their functions until relieved by the first Board of Visitors for the University of Virginia.

The first meeting of these latter took place on the 29th of March, 1819.   There were present Thomas Jefferson, who was elected Rector, James Madison, Joseph C. Cabell, Chapman Johnson, James Breckinridge, Robert Taylor and John H. Cocke.   After having elected a proctor and a bursar, and having chosen a common seal, they enacted sundry provisions as to the salaries of the professors which need not occupy us here; but one entry on the minutes is important enough to quote:

"That Dr. Thomas Cooper, of Philadelphia, heretofore appointed professor of chemistry and of law for the Central College, be confirmed and appointed for the University as professor of chemistry, mineralogy and natural philosophy, and as professor of law also until the advance of the institution and the increase of the number of students shall render necessary a separate appointment to the professorship of law. . . ."

Then follows a statement that it is both important and difficult to get American citizens as professors, and Thomas Jefferson and John H. Cocke are appointed a Committee of Superintendence to secure such provisionally—all actual engagements being deferred until the Board shall meet.

The report of Cooper's election being now noised abroad through the state, the sectional feeling before alluded to not

[1] For a subsequent scheme of establishing a chair of agriculture, the duties of which were finally assigned to the professor of chemistry, see Madison's Writings, III, 284-7.

having been allayed, and the politicians fearing that Jefferson had entrapped them into a new way to spend money for which they would be held responsible, a terrific outcry arose that Atheism was to be publicly taught, that the state would become bankrupt, that the good old times were gone forever, and that war was being waged against the manhood and virtue of Virginia by the arch-scoffer of Monticello, seconded by his deistical follower of Montpellier. The hue and cry was as loud as it was silly. As is often the case, "base political tricksters" joined with really honest and well-minded clergymen in this war of words and pamphlets. The result will be seen in the record of the meeting of the Visitors on October 4, 1819, where the duties of Dr. Cooper's professorship are deferred and the Committee of Superintendence directed to arrange with him the terms on which such postponement may be made *conformable to honor* and without inconveniencing him. The non-completion of the buildings and Cooper's own offer to resign furnished a plausible plea for this treatment; and we see from the Rector's report for November 29th, 1821, that Cooper, who in the meantime had been made president of the Columbia, S. C., College, compromised for $1,500. So ended the Cooper episode, not very pleasantly for any of the parties concerned.[1] I have paid attention to it because it is of considerable importance to my main theme, which might be called not inaptly "The evolution of the University of Virginia's professorships."[2]

---

[1] But even as late as January, 1824, Jefferson had not wholly given up the idea of getting Cooper, nor had that gentleman himself lost hope. See Madison's Writings, III, 360.

[2] It may be remarked here once for all that no questions were asked as to the religious opinions of any of those who first filled chairs in the University. The agent who was sent to England did not mention the subject until it was broached to him. All of the first faculty seem to have been Episcopalians except Dr. Blaetterman, who was a Lutheran. See Randall, III, 467–8. It is curious that John Adams opposed the selection of foreign professors because they would teach Christianity. See his works, X, 415.

I have not the space, even if I had the inclination, to describe the woes and tribulations which the friends of the university underwent for the next four years. Every fresh demand for money was received with a groan by the legislature. Men forgot that not one private house in a hundred is built for anything like the first estimate, and they accused Mr. Jefferson of everything a scurrilous politician knows himself to be guilty of. But the philosopher stood it all, though sorely tried at times. He was out of the thick of the fight, as a general should be, but his lieutenant, Cabell, was doing manful work in Richmond, a city opposed to Mr. Jefferson on principle, and hence inveterately hostile to the new university. Even those who were not hostile despaired of its success, and the majority Cabell could count on in the legislature showed signs of becoming a minority. Finally one great move was made by the foe—this was no less than to remove William and Mary to Richmond and give the old college another chance in connection with a medical school which would have clinical advantages Charlottesville could not give. This was a side blow to the University, and an almost deadly one. "What!" its advocates would say, "Here you have had oceans of money given you by the state, and you begrudge setting this historic college on its feet again!" And so the columns of the *Enquirer* for 1824 were filled with contributions signed by "Friends of the State," "Friends of learning," "Constant Readers," and other representatives of a class that unfortunately still survives. But Cabell and his stout phalanx, among whom was Dr. Rice, reconciled now that Cooper was put out of the way, won the day in spite of the opposing odds. The president of William and Mary had to wend his sad way homeward, and the college which had partially revived under his management drooped finally forever.[1]

---

[1] This was written before the scheme for the rehabilitation of the noble old college appeared to have any chance of success. Under its present

But in the meantime something was doing which concerns us more nearly, something as important as anything which Jefferson had planned or Cabell executed.

Reference has been made to the fact that the Board had seen the wisdom of conciliating public opinion by securing native professors. But they were determined to have none but good ones. All their outlay would have been to little purpose if the professors chosen were but ordinary men; and so the selection of professors was by far the most difficult task that lay before them. They were prompt in their action. On the 3d of October, 1820, they resolved that negotiations should be entered into with " the following persons with the view of engaging them as professors of the University, viz., Mr. Bowditch, of Salem,[1] and Mr. Ticknor, of Boston."[2] The compensation to be given them was ample, considering the data of the offer; it consisted of apartments, of a regular salary of $2,000 per annum, of a fee of $10 from each student in their classes, and an engagement on the part of the University to see that the sum total of $2,500 should be secured to them for the first three years.[3] For reasons best known to themselves these gentlemen declined and, as Mr. Jefferson

---

efficient management there seems to be no reason why William and Mary should not live forever to connect modern generations with those old times of which we are so proud. Certainly the friends of the University of Virginia can afford not to be jealous and to lend all their help to the meritorious enterprise, and certainly the thanks of all Virginians are due to the Bureau of Education for the monograph which turned the light of modern educational science upon the time-honored institution.

[1] Nathaniel Bowditch (1773–1838), the well-known mathematician and navigator, and translator of Laplace's "Mécanique Céleste," refused professorships in Harvard and West Point as well.

[2] Ticknor's visit to Monticello in 1815 had made a deep impression on Mr. Jefferson, and is more than once mentioned in the Gilmer letters. See Ticknor's Life and Letters, I, 34, 300, 302. Both these nominations seem to have excited the displeasure of the religious opponents of Cooper. See Adams' Thomas Jefferson on p. 71.

[3] Jefferson-Cabell Correspondence, page 460.

had probably foreseen from the start, the University was forced to look abroad for a majority of its first professors. This naturally brought up two questions, how many professors were to be gotten, and who was to choose them. The Board some time before had determined that only eight professors could be employed at first, for the fund at their disposal had not proved too ample for the buildings, and economy was necessary on all sides. Mr. Jefferson and Mr. Madison, with him, thought that two of these professorships could not well be intrusted to foreign hands—those of ethics and law—but that the other six had better be filled from England. This was proposed to the members of the Board by letter and elicited the following response from Mr. Cabell.

BREMO,[1] *April* 16, 1824.

* * * .

I was very much pleased at the limitation of the foreign professors to a moiety of the whole number. I thought I could see advantages in this limitation, which I attempted to explain to the Board of Visitors. I need not repeat what I said upon this subject. The Professor of Anatomy is not like the Professor of Law and Politics, and the Professor of Ethics, connected with a science calculated to give tone and direction to the public mind, on the most important subjects that can occupy the human understanding. It is of the class of Professorships which may be prudently filled by foreigners. For this reason, and because the difference between five and six is but one; and above all, because you are an infinitely better judge of the subject than I am, and it is my greatest happiness to give you pleasure upon any and upon all occasions, you may consider me as yielding my assent to your

---

[1] Bremo was Gen. Cocke's county seat in Fluvanna. For this letter see the Jefferson-Cabell Correspondence, page 303.

3

proposition to instruct the agent to engage the Anatomical
Professor in Europe. . . .   Yours,

JOSEPH C. CABELL.

I concur with Mr. Cabell in the above.

JOHN H. COCKE.

The first question having been satisfactorily answered, the
second pressed for solution.   Mr. Jefferson's first choice of a
commissioner who should proceed to England to procure the
necessary professors, naturally fell upon the man who had
stood by him so nobly and so faithfully—Joseph C. Cabell.
But Mr. Cabell's affairs were embarrassed, for he had purchased a large portion of his brother's property which would
be a dead loss unless it received his immediate personal attention; besides he needed rest, and moreover had another
scheme on his hands—a canal to connect the eastern and
western waters.   So he was forced to decline this commission,
honorable and confidential as it was.   Then Mr. Jefferson
rode over to Mr. Madison's and they consulted long and
earnestly about the matter.   This was in November, 1823.
Finally Mr. Cabell was consulted and doubtless others of the
Board, and then Mr. Jefferson wrote to a young lawyer in
Richmond requesting his presence at Monticello on urgent
business.   The antecedents of that young lawyer must now
engage our attention. [1]

---

[1] Much of the preceding chapter is necessarily a recapitulation of what
Dr. Adams has so well and so fully presented in his recent monograph.   I
must add, however, in justice to myself, that the chapter was written several months before I was enabled to consult Dr. Adams' work.   I have,
therefore, travelled over the same ground independently, and can testify,
were testimony needed, to the thoroughness and accuracy of his researches
and conclusions.

CHAPTER II.

FRANCIS WALKER GILMER.

Francis Walker Gilmer was the youngest child of Dr. George Gilmer, of Pen Park, Albemarle County, Virginia. He was born on the ninth day of October in the year seventeen hundred and ninety, or rather Francis *Thornton* Gilmer was born on that day, for so the young child was christened. He did not assume the name Francis Walker until after the death of an uncle of that name—an event which happened somewhere about the year 1808.[1] The Gilmers are of Scotch extraction, and settled in this country in 1731.[2] They have always held a high and honorable position, and many members of the family have been distinguished for more than usual intellect. They have given Virginia a Governor and the United States a Cabinet Minister in the person of Thomas Walker Gilmer, Governor of Virginia (1840–41) and member of Congress, who was killed just after his appointment as Secretary of the Navy, by the bursting of a gun on board the " Princeton " in February, 1844. The victim of this tragedy, which deprived Virginia of two of her most eminent men, was the nephew of the subject of my sketch.

---

[1] This may have been the Francis Walker who was a representative in Congress 1793–1795; but the point is uncertain.

[2] For a good account of the Gilmers see "Sketches of some of the First Settlers of Upper Georgia," by Gov. George R. Gilmer (New York, Appleton, 1855). The Gilmers settled in Georgia after the Revolution, and the author of the above-mentioned book was one of the most noted members of the family.

27

I do not think that the genealogy of the family with a long string of names and dates is essential to my purpose, but a few words descriptive of Mr. Gilmer's father will not be out of place—for the son was said to have inherited, in no small degree, his father's temperament and talents. Now, for such a description, I can go to no better person than William Wirt, Dr. Gilmer's son-in-law. In a letter to Francis, written from Richmond on the 9th of October, 1806, Mr. Wirt speaks as follows :—" You, I understand, propose to follow your father's profession. The science of medicine is, I believe, said to be progressive and to be daily receiving new improvements—you will, therefore, have a wider field to cultivate, and will take the profession on a grander scale—it will be your own fault, therefore, if you do not, as a physician, 'fill a larger space in the public eye.' But the space which your father occupied was not filled merely by his eminence as a physician (although he was certainly among the most eminent), he was moreover a very good linguist—a master of botany and the chemistry of his day—had a store of very correct general science—was a man of superior taste in the fine arts—and to crown the whole, had an elevated and a noble spirit, and was in his manners and conversation a most accomplished gentleman—easy and graceful in his movements, eloquent in speech, a temper gay and animated, and inspiring every company with its own tone—wit pure, sparkling and perennial—and when the occasion called for it, sentiments of the highest dignity and utmost force. Such was your father before disease had sapped his mind and constitution—and such the model which, as your brother, I would wish you to adopt. It will be a model much more easy for you to form yourself on than any other, because it will be natural to you—for I well remember to have remarked, when you were scarcely four years old, how strongly nature had given you the cast of your father's character." [1]

---

[1] This letter is one of the many from Wirt to Gilmer, given in Kennedy's Life of Wirt. I had intended to append a special dissertation, showing

Mr. Wirt spoke warmly, and he had reason so to do. He had come poor and friendless into a strange state, and the Gilmers had taken him by the hand. His humble birth was forgotten and, in 1795, he married Mildred, the eldest daughter of the house. Pen Park, the Doctor's country seat, was near Monticello, and the master of the house, having himself served the Revolution well, was the intimate friend of Thomas Jefferson.[1] Living at this hospitable home with his young bride, Wirt was thrown with Jefferson and Madison and Monroe, with the Barbours and the Carrs. The youngest Carr, Dabney, son of Dabney, was ever after his dearest friend. Of him we shall have to speak many times.

But troubles came upon the house. Dr. Gilmer died shortly after the marriage of his daughter, and the latter did not long survive him. Wirt, cast adrift upon the world after many wanderings, settled down in Richmond to achieve a well-earned fame. Pen Park passed out of the family, and the brothers were scattered. Peachy, the eldest of the surviving

---

how Kennedy wilfully altered these letters; but I find that I can only allude to the fact briefly. Allowing for mistakes that might have been made in copying, I find abundant proof that Kennedy took it upon himself to improve the style of Wirt's letters, although he did not tamper much with the matter. He did not succeed in this gratuitous task. The original letters are far less tame than the epistles which have been substituted for them. Frequently whole sentences are omitted, with no asterisks to mark that the text is not continuous. Two of the letters are misdated, phrases are often transposed or dropped, and in one letter, of which only half the original is given, I count upwards of twenty-three variations. It is needless to say that Wirt was not the man to use strong terms unless he meant them. Mr. Kennedy has not thought fit to leave any of the few expressions which show that Wirt was after all a man like ourselves. He does, however, leave the letter in which Wirt made the curious mistake of attributing to Beattie or Dryden the majestic passage from Gray's "Progress of Poesy," beginning "Now the rich stream of music winds along." This mistake is rendered all the more curious by the fact that Wirt was fond of repeating "The Bard."

[1] Dr. Gilmer left certain manuscripts relating to the Revolution. These have been edited by R. A. Brock, and published in one of the late volumes of the Virginia Historical Society Papers.

children, settled far away in Henry County to the great disgust of his friends who thought that his many talents deserved a wider field.   James, another promising son, died just as he was about to build up a law practice at Charlottesville. Harmer and Francis, the two younger, were left to get what education they could in a county where good schools flourished not.   The guardian of Francis (and I presume Harmer's also) acted an ignoble part by them and, if I chose to present the pitiful letters of the former, written in his sixteenth year, I could give this chapter a very mournful cast.   The boy's training was almost entirely neglected, and though he had property of his own, he got little good from it during his minority.   But he had a few warm friends.   The family at Monticello offered all the help a proud nature was willing to accept.   Mrs. Randolph taught him French and he grew up and played with her children, and even then Mr. Jefferson noted the brilliancy of his mind and prophesied great things of him.

His letters of this period (1806) are interesting, for they give us glimpses of a fine character gradually moulding itself under circumstances as adverse as possible.   Now he describes his forlorn position; now he gives us his opinion of the books he has been reading; now he tells how kind the Monticello people are.   He does not like Pope's Homer for the time-honored reason that Pope is not Homer; but he nearly cried over the episode of Nisus and Euryalus.   Anacreon is not much to his fancy, but he delights in Cæsar's Commentaries and thinks they are " very easy."

But in 1807 a brighter tone appears.   A Mr. Ogilvie is going to have a fine classical school at Milton (a small hamlet near Charlottesville), and he will at last have a chance to make a man of himself.   Alas! this hope fails him, for the aspiring Ogilvie cannot content himself with two scholars.

I fear my readers will accuse me of being a man of many digressions, but I cannot refrain from a passing notice of this eccentric character who became a correspondent of Gil-

mer's. He was a Scotchman of good family and was born
about 1775.[1] Emigrating to this country he taught a school
in Richmond where he was very successful in stimulating his
pupils with a love for study, although his own mind was too
unbalanced to have imparted much solid information. Some
of his pupils were afterwards distinguished—a writer in the
Southern Literary Messenger (Vol. XIV, p. 534), enumerat-
ing Gen. Winfield Scott, Hon. W. S. Archer, Gov. Duvall,
of Florida Territory, and possibly Thomas Ritchie, the editor
of the Richmond *Enquirer*. Whether this Richmond success
came before or after the Milton failure, I am unable to say,
as the dates are rather mixed. But Ogilvie was not destined
to be a "drudge of a schoolmaster;" he conceived the laudable and lofty design of enlightening the American people
upon the principles of *"true oratory"* and of *"philosophical
criticism."* But such a task required arduous preparation,
and he accordingly retired from South Carolina where he had
been on some wild goose chase, to the backwoods of Kentucky,
there to meditate and woo the Muse of Eloquence. Whether
it was for this latter end that he joined a volunteer expedition
against the Indians, I know not; but the account he gives of
that expedition, in a letter to Gilmer, is worthy of preserva-
tion. It must, however, be condemned to lie among its companion MSS. until I can find a fitter opportunity to give it to
the world. Having encountered no Indians, the philan-
thropist retired to a lonely log house, stipulating with his
landlady that he was to see no company—a rather unnecessary precaution it would seem. Here in the winter of 1812–13
was composed a series of orations which were shortly afterwards delivered in Philadelphia, New York and Boston. In
spite of his erratic religious opinions his success was remarkable. The American people were evidently willing to be

[1] The biographical dictionaries give the date of his birth variously. I
ascertained from one of his letters that the date I have given is the
right one.

instructed in the principles of oratory and of philosophical criticism, whether the instruction profited much or little. The letter in which he describes his success is worthy of this peripatetic from the Athens of Scotland to the Athens of America. Among his auditors in New York was Francis Jeffrey. In Boston young George Ticknor thought him a wonderful elocutionist.[1] But the use of narcotics was gradually destroying his mind. A volume of his essays was received with derision; and having heard of the death of his relative, the Earl of Finlater and Airy, without near heirs, he determined to go to Scotland and put in his own claim for the title. He failed and died at Aberdeen in 1820, presumably by his own hand. He is said to have done much harm to the cause of religion and morality in Virginia; of this I have no evidence. His pupils spoke of him with affection, and his influence on young Gilmer was probably confined to stimulating him in the study of the classics and to giving him a bent toward public life; for, as we have seen above, the latter had at one time proposed to become a physician.

But although Francis was thus disappointed in his expectation of becoming a pupil of this curious man, something better was in store for him. Through the efforts and advice of Mr. William A. Burwell, long a member of Congress from the Bedford district, and a firm friend of the Gilmers, the boy, now in his eighteenth year and the possessor of a vast amount of ill-sorted information, was placed at a school in Georgetown where he would be under Mr. Burwell's eye. This was in the winter of 1808–9. In the fall of 1809 he entered William and Mary College and remained there for a session. Mr. Wirt says that he met him there for the first time since his childhood, and that "in point of learning he was already a prodigy." He adds:[2] "His learning, indeed, was of a curious cast: for

---

[1] Ticknor's Life, &c., I, 8.

[2] This is taken from Wirt's preface to the Baltimore edition of Gilmer's Sketches, to be mentioned hereafter.

having had no one to direct his studies, he seems to have
devoured indiscriminately everything that came in his way.
He had been removed from school to school, in different parts
of the country—had met at all these places with different collections of old books, of which he was always fond, and seemed
also to have had command of his father's medical library,
which he had read in the original Latin.   It was curious to
hear a boy of seventeen years of age [he was over nineteen]
speaking with fluency and even with manly eloquence, and
quoting such names as Boerhaave, Van Helmont, Van Swei-
ten, together with Descartes, Gassendi, Newton, Locke, and
descanting on the system of Linnaeus with the familiarity of
a veteran professor.   He lived, however, to reduce this *chaos*
to order, and was, before he died, as remarkable for the digested
method as the extent and accuracy of his attainments."

Such was the impression made by this remarkable youth
that Bishop Madison, then president of the college, offered him
the ushership of the grammar school connected with the institution, but the offer was declined ; for the young man was
bent upon public life.   Among Gilmer's classmates was George
Croghan, of Kentucky (1791–1849), destined to become a hero
in the war of 1812 ; they seem to have had some correspondence after the termination of hostilities, but only one letter of
Croghan's has been preserved.

In 1811 we find that Mr. Wirt had invited Gilmer to read
law with him in Richmond ; and now follow some of the
pleasantest years of his life.   Wirt was at that time at the
head of the Richmond bar, and his "Letters of a British Spy"
had given him a national renown.   He had married into a
distinguished family (the Gambles), and was able to introduce
his protegé to a large and cultivated circle of friends—to
Wickham and Hay and Call [1] and Dr. McClurg,[2] to Tazewell

---

[1] All leading lawyers, the latter was reporter for the Court of Appeals.
[2] A finely educated physician, and a member of the Philadelphia Conven-
tion of 1787.

whenever he came to practice in the Court of Appeals, to
ex-Gov. now Judge Wm. H. Cabell, who entertained most of
the strangers of distinction that visited Richmond, to Dr. Rice,
of whom we have heard before; to Dr. Brokenborough, the
life-long friend of John Randolph, and last but not least, to
William Pope, the prince of good fellows, who lived about
twenty miles from Richmond, but whose jokes were known
from one end of the state to the other. Pope was the man
who, whenever he came to Richmond, went to Wirt's office to
hear select passages read from the " Life of Patrick Henry,"
and did nothing but weep during the performance.

Here, then, was some compensation for the dreariness of his
early life. We catch glimpses of his progress through Black-
stone, on to Mansfield and Erskine, and finally, O dreary task!
to the Virginia Reporters. We hear his opinions of different
reigning belles and of the last doings of Napoleon; we find
him rejoicing at his providential escape from the burning of
the Richmond Theatre; and finally we come full upon vivid
descriptions of the horror felt in Richmond at the reports of
Cockburn's raid.

In the militia movements of the state during this trouble-
some time Gilmer took his share. In the camp below Richmond, near Warrenigh Church, he drilled daily with his
friends the Carrs and young Jefferson Randolph. His fellow
student in the law, Abel P. Upshur, was also there, not destined to be shot by the British, but to rise to be Secretary of
the Navy and of State, and to perish in the accident on board
the Princeton. But the British would not come in spite of
the fact that brave and irascible Colonel Thomas Mann Randolph (Jefferson's son-in-law) was waiting for them ; and the
passage from Tyrtaeus, which he had copied out in the Greek
and given to Gilmer, did no good at all. What wonder then
that the warlike Colonel, afterwards Governor, knocked a
gentleman down for alluding to this abortive campaign !

Flesh and blood could not stand a camp before which no
enemy was to be seen, and so we find Gilmer and Upshur

tossing away their guns and sallying homeward, leaving Captain Wirt, with his flying company of artillery, to write soothing letters to Mrs. W. and to curse his own position.

In the meantime young Harmer Gilmer, who had taken his medical degree at Philadelphia, and was looking forward to following in his father's footsteps, was taken ill at Charlottesville and died. Francis was with him and nursed him faithfully, although his own health was far from good. He had always been slight and frail, and the air of Richmond did not agree with him. And now that his companion brother had been taken away from him, the clouds that lowered over the whole country seemed to be blackest over his own devoted head.

But with him, as with all of us, time and change of scene wrought a cure. We pass over his snubbing Wirt's attempts at Comedy (Kennedy, I, 351), and the gay days spent at Montevideo, Judge Cabell's residence in Buckingham, and find him at last fully determined to begin the practice of the law in Winchester. He had previously thought of settling in Lexington, Kentucky; but, as with subsequent schemes, the thought of leaving his mother state, now that she seemed in a precarious condition, unnerved him and he resolved to stay. Not the least interesting part of these letters is the constant reference to the financial affairs of Virginia from 1815 to 1830. They show an utter despair of improvement, from the complete relapse, suffered after the war of 1812, and from the load of debt then sorely pressing upon the older families. The troubles that came upon Mr. Jefferson have become historic, but I could mention other cases to show that the current opinion that Virginia was ruined by the late war is utterly erroneous. Virginia was ruined long before, ruined by an extravagant system of labor, by a lavish hospitality, by inattention to ordinary business principles. The war only hastened the crisis a few years.

Gilmer's plan of settlement was made in April, 1814; but in September of that year his schemes had not been matured, owing to the unsettled state of the country. In the meantime he had been exercising his pen in the production of certain essays—having now locked up among his treasures a manuscript volume of "Physical and Moral Essays," some of which afterwards saw the light. As a few of his literary productions are of consequence in themselves, and as all are of consequence in enabling us to inform ourselves of his character, I shall in this chapter simply note the date and title of such as were published, and shall defer all discussion of their merits until a subsequent chapter in which I hope to examine the character of the man and his work in some detail.

It was during this summer that he became acquainted, or at least developed an intimacy with that wonderful old philosopher, the Abbé Corrèa. With the exception of Mr. Jefferson this man did more to form Gilmer's character than did any other of his distinguished friends. Joseph Francisco Corrèa de Serra was born in Portugal in 1750. He studied at Rome and Naples, was admitted to holy orders, and returned to Portugal in 1777. Here he took great interest in the foundation of the Lisbon Academy, and in 1779 was made its perpetual secretary. He did an excellent work while connected with this institution in collecting cabinets of specimens—chiefly botanical, and in editing numerous unpublished documents relative to early Portuguese history. But he did not escape the suspicions of the Inquisition, and in 1786 it became necessary for him to seek refuge in Paris. There he continued his studies and contracted an intimacy with the naturalist Broussonnet. After the death of Pedro III, Corrèa returned to his native country, and to him Broussonnet fled on the outbreak of the Reign of Terror. Rendered an object of suspicion by his hospitality to the exile, Corrèa found it necessary to go into hiding himself; for the authorities, under the direction of a tyrannical intendant-general of police, were busily engaged in crushing out all democratic tendencies. After a retreat to London, about 1796, Corrèa was employed in a diplomatic relation at Paris, where he

remained from 1802 to 1813. In the latter year he embarked
for the United States and, coming to Philadelphia, was engaged
to deliver lectures on botany in the University of that city.
He was subsequently appointed Portuguese minister to this
country. Like all foreigners he was attracted to Mr. Jefferson
and became a frequent inmate at Monticello where, in all probability, Francis Gilmer first met him. The Abbé was drawn
toward the young Virginian by the latter's enthusiasm for
all science—especially for botany. We have heard how Mr.
Wirt found him discoursing on Linnaeus at Williamsburg,
and it appears from his letters that he had since gone deeper
into the subject. He was familiar with the flora of most of
the sections of his native state, and he was now destined under
the guidance of Mr. Corrèa to make vast acquisitions to his
knowledge. But I shall let him describe his new friend in
his own words, which are taken from a letter written by him
to his brother Peachy Gilmer on the 3d of November, 1814:

"I am so far [Richmond] on my way to Philadelphia with
Mr. Corrèa, of whom, I dare say, you heard me speak of last
summer. He is the most extraordinary man now living, or
who, perhaps, ever lived. None of the ancient or modern
languages; none of the sciences, physical or moral; none of
the appearances of earth, air, or ocean, stand him any more
chance than the Pope of Rome, as old Jonett[1] used to say. I
have never heard him asked a question which he could not
answer; never seen him in company with a man who did not
appear to be a fool to him; never heard him make a remark
which ought not to be remembered. He has read, seen, understands and remembers everything contained in books, or to be
learned by travel, observation, and the conversation of learned
men. He is a member of every philosophical society in the
world, and knows every distinguished man living, &c." Making all due allowances, we must, nevertheless, admit that the

---

[1] I do not know who is referred to.

man who could so impress a young man rather given to cyni-
cism than otherwise, was no ordinary personage.

The journey to Philadelphia was taken, and Gilmer pro-
nounced the months spent there the happiest of his life.
He contracted intimacies with John Vaughan, Secretary of
the Philosophical Society, with Dr. Caspar Wistar, afterwards
president of that society, and connected with the abolition
movement, with Robert Walsh, the *littérateur*, and with young
George Ticknor, then opening his eyes at the magnificence of
Philadelphia dinner parties. He was probably present at the
very dinner where John Randolph, in defending the gentlemen of Virginia from an imaginary insult from Mr. Corrèa,
forgot, as he so often did, to be a gentleman himself.[1] But he
had to tear himself away at last, even from the fascinations of
a certain belle who is not infrequently mentioned in the letters
written about this time. The visit not only left pleasant
memories but led to various correspondences which will be
mentioned in due course, but which cannot be enlarged upon.
It also led to a great scheme, mysterious and all engrossing,
the particulars of which I have not been able to make out,
but which shows that the young man of twenty-four was still
enthusiastic. It is a scheme of travel in Europe with Mr.
Corrèa, from which large revenues are in some way to flow—
but the aforesaid revenues would not begin flowing out until
a thousand dollars were poured in, which thousand dollars
Peachy Gilmer was conjured to bring with him to Albemarle.
But luckily or unluckily for our schemers, Napoleon came
back from Elba and set Europe in a blaze, which the philosophic Corrèa, now aged 65, did not care to pass through, and
so this mysterious quest of El Dorado in the old world was
abandoned, and Mr. Gilmer settled down in Winchester about
the first of August, 1815. But he had not begun to practice
before the old Abbé was on him again, this time come to per-

---

[1] Ticknor's Life and Letters, I, 16.

suade him to take an expedition through the Carolinas for botanizing purposes. The temptation was too strong; the young lawyer was so highly flattered by the evident fondness of the great man for him, and his scientific ardor was so kindled, that the shingle freshly hung out was taken down and the two enthusiasts started off. I leave the reader to imagine the pleasure Gilmer found in seeing new places and new faces, and in learning a favorite science under such a teacher; I must myself hurry on in my narrative.

Winchester now became Gilmer's abode for the next two years. There he found a respectable bar, and what was better, three staunch friends—Dabney Carr, Henry St. George Tucker, and Judge Holmes. Dabney Carr was, as we have already seen, the great friend of William Wirt, and the favorite nephew of Thomas Jefferson. He was now in his forty-fourth year, and was Chancellor for the Winchester district. He was an amiable and intelligent man, and did much to direct the young practitioner in his studies. Tucker was then member of Congress for his district, and his letters written to Gilmer from Washington are not the least interesting in this correspondence. These two, together with Judge Holmes and Mr. Wirt, helped to make Gilmer the most learned lawyer for his age in Virginia.

It is interesting to read of his successful defence of a horse-thief who was notoriously guilty; of the six cases which this one success brought him; of his schemes for future glory, and of his endeavors to overcome certain natural impediments to fluent speaking; but I am reminded of the more important work to be done, and regretfully pass over much of more than usual interest. It must, however, be mentioned that just about this time (1816) a Baltimore printer gave to the world a pamphlet containing sketches of certain American orators, which was much talked about in Washington, and was attributed to Mr. Wirt. But a few weeks later the rumor spread abroad, greatly to Gilmer's disgust, that Mr. Wirt's favorite pupil, and not Mr. Wirt himself, was the author. The guilty young critic could not deny the charge, and gained an enviable reputation in Virginia as a coming man of letters.

In the meantime Gilmer was corresponding with Ticknor, who was now in Göttingen writing warm letters about the progress of German science, and sage letters as to his friend's keeping up his health; with Hugh S. Legaré, whom he had met on his southern trip, and who gives us glimpses of the methods of study which were to lead to his future distinction— with Corrèa, the omniscient, whose careful handwriting it is a pleasure to read; with Mr. Wirt, in answer to that gentleman's elegant epistles of advice; with Tucker in Congress; and with Mr. Jefferson, on subjects of political economy, also on the subject of the boundaries of Lousiana, on which he was writing an article. Jefferson replied that although soon after the acquisition of that country, he had minutely investigated its history and " formed a memoir establishing its boundaries from Perdido to the Rio Bravo" (which papers were sent to the American Commissioner at Madrid, copies remaining, however, in the Secretary of State's office), he had now no documents by him that could help Gilmer. He, however, referred him to an article in the " Virginia Argus," of some time in January, 1816, which was so free from errors that he suspected that some one in the Secretary of State's office must have written it. Gilmer corresponded also with the celebrated Du Pont de Nemours (1739–1817), who, after a varied and brilliant life at the French court, had come to New Jersey in 1802 and, disdaining all Napoleon's offers, had resolved to turn his talents to account among a fresh young people— neglecting, however, to learn their language, though he lived among them for fifteen years. Respecting this last correspondence, we will quote a few words from a letter to Mr. Wirt:

" Mr. Corrèa has put me to corresponding with the celebrated Du Pont (de Nemours), who writes the longest letters in French and in the worst hand I ever saw; he writes often, and the correspondence occupies a good deal of my leisure. I shall transcribe his letters in a book, and when we live to quit the bars and courts and study the history of the strange things which have passed before us, we will read them together."

It will always be one of the regrets of my life that Gilmer did not transcribe the aforesaid letters, for many a weary hour did I spend deciphering them—to find nothing after all very worthy of my pains. They are filled with reflections upon our government not particularly profound—unless the fact that my eyes were nearly blinded by the strain to which they were subjected, blinded my critical powers—with panegyrics on Quesnay and Turgot, whom by the way he induced Gilmer to read, and thus deserves our thanks,[1] with compliments to Gilmer and invitations to him to undertake a translation of a certain treatise on Education, which he had written for the benefit of this uneducated country ; with lamentations over the state of France, where the clerical party were beginning that reaction which cost the Bourbons their throne; and with encomiums upon Mr. Jefferson in spite of the fact that that philosopher had allowed the distinguished Frenchman to visit him for a week without once seeing him ;[2] from all of which I excerpt one passage and hasten on :

---

[1] In this connection I must quote the following from a letter to Wirt: " In economy the French have opened one window and the English another on the opposite side (as the Chevalier Corrèa says), but nobody has seen more than an apartment of the great edifice."

[2] Extract from a letter written by Gilmer to Wirt dated Winchester, January, 1816.

" By the way, this puts me in mind to ask you if the worthy St. Thomas of Canterbury has ever written to you concerning the *clari oratores.* I have always forgotten to mention to you in my letters that I made the application to him, and he treated it as Pope [William Pope, before mentioned] says, in a 'particular manner.' That I might leave a kind of lasting memento to jog his memory, I wrote him a very polite note, mentioning the subject in the best way I could, to which he did me the honor to return no answer, and the matter ended, as I did not think it proper considering the anti-duelling laws to challenge him, as J. Randolph would probably have done. If he has not written to you on the subject, you need take it as no particular negligence towards yourself, as he lately suffered the celebrated

4

"Such is the system of your elections, imitated from those of England, whose central point is the tavern where Madame Intrigue solicits, pays for and obtains the protection of My Lord Whiskey. You haven't yet got to giving one another blows over the head with great sticks, or to detaching the shoulders from the body with ——(?) as is done at London and Westminster; but already blows of the fist are not spared, and the chiefs of opinion have themselves accompanied by two body-guards—vigorous *Boxers.* This evil may be less great in your Virginia, and it is less great because you have there another evil graver still—all manual labor is done by slaves who have not and who ought not to have a voice in elections. It is to this same evil that you owe, with some justice, what is called 'the Virginian Dynasty.'"

These letters from Du Pont occasioned considerable correspondence between Gilmer and Mr. Jefferson, for the old courtier's French was beyond the dictionaries at Winchester. The treatise on Education was translated, but, for various reasons, was not given to the world.[1]

But the young lawyer was longing for a wider field. He was doing well at Winchester, had in fact made his expenses the first year; but this by no means satisfied him. So Attorney-General Wirt and Chancellor Carr were consulted as to

---

Du Pont de Nemours, a grave senator of France, near 80 years of age to visit him at Monticello, stay a week and not see him."

Gilmer refers above to the fact that Wirt found some difficulty in getting Jefferson's opinion as to his life of Patrick Henry. There is another characteristic sentence of Gilmer's on this subject which I take from a letter to Wirt, written on the 16th of December, 1816: "The old citizen of Monticello is such a diplomatist that he has quite baffled our schemes to obtain his opinion; and when we ask him one thing he tells us he 'has reason to believe' something about another. A plague upon all diplomacy, I say."

[1] The French version was published in Paris and had gone through a second edition by 1812. It is to be hoped that Gilmer had the printed book to translate from. For a synopsis of this treatise which is said to have influenced Jefferson's ideas on higher education, see Adams' *Thomas Jefferson, &c.,* pp. 49, 50, 51.

his future location. Wirt decidedly favored Baltimore, but it
was found that a rule of court required a three years residence
in Maryland, and this unfair protection of native intellect
forced the aspirant for legal fame to make a Napoleonic dash,
as Wirt called it, to Richmond. This was in the winter of
1817–18.

His first impressions of Richmond were not favorable, and
he, therefore, made a flying trip to Baltimore to see whether
the rule could not be broken down. Some of his friends there
were convinced that an exception would be made in his case;
and as Pinckney was likely to be out of the way, either in
Russia or in Washington, under the government, there seemed
to be a fine opening. But these things were uncertain, and
Gilmer returned to Richmond, where, after an abortive attempt
to induce some of his friends to go with him to Florida, he
finally settled with something like content. It may be noted
that he made some endeavors, through Mr. Wirt, to obtain the
secretaryship of state for the new territory of Florida; but
Mr. Monroe decidedly discouraged the application on the
ground that Gilmer ought not to think of thus burying himself—a fact which served to increase the young man's dislike
to the "most popular president."

Not long after his return to Richmond, he was appointed
by the court to defend one Gibson, who had committed a most
atrocious and open murder. The man was convicted, but
Gilmer got him a new trial on two nice legal points, and so,
in the opinion of his friends, obtained a great victory. We
also hear incidentally of a thousand dollar fee for recovering
some land in Orange County, of a trip to Georgia for a similar
purpose, and of sundry claims given him by Robert Walsh—
all of which tends to show that he was by no means idle. Nor
was there any lack of appreciation of his work on the part of
his friends and acquaintances. There were rumors that President Smith of William and Mary was to be called to Philadelphia in Dr. Wistar's place, and a letter to Jefferson, of
March 18th, 1818, hints that Gilmer might be asked to

become the head of his *alma mater.* Jefferson replied on
April 10th: "I trust you did not for a moment seriously
think of shutting yourself behind the door of William and
Mary College. A more complete *cul de sac* could not be proposed to you."[1] We also see from a letter to his brother
Peachy, written about a year later, that he stood some chance
of being made Attorney General of Virginia.

During this time also (1819-20) he had a correspondence
with Benjamin Vaughan (brother to John, of Philadelphia),
the antiquarian of Hallowell, Maine, who after many years of
good works in England, continued the same in this country
until his death in 1835. Vaughan lent him a copy of Smith's
General History of Virginia (London Edition, 1629), and the
result was that Gilmer induced Dr. Rice to publish the first
American edition of this valuable work in 1819. Nor was
he idle in the law. He was appointed by the Court of Appeals
to report their decisions, and published a thin volume of
reports in 1821; but the legislature did not make the office
of Reporter profitable enough, and he only served one year.

In the meantime George Hay, a distinguished Richmond
lawyer, Monroe's son-in-law, and the prosecutor of Aaron
Burr, had published a work against usury laws. Gilmer had
read Bentham and the Edinburgh Reviewers on the subject,
and disagreeing, published a reply to *them,* disdaining to notice
Mr. Hay's performance. This production of his thirtieth year
gained many high commendations from such men as Mr. Jefferson, John Randolph of Roanoke. Mr. Wirt, and Rufus King.

From a letter of June 26th, 1820, we find that he was not
unknown abroad. A young friend, Dabney Carr Terrell, who
had been studying in Geneva, brought him a letter from De
Caudolle, the celebrated professor of botany at that University, in which the savan solicited specimens from America, and
promised that any observations Gilmer might make should be

inserted and acknowledged in the great work to which he was devoting his life. The postscript to this letter is as follows:

" It is worth while to mention, too, as an honor done me abroad for what was hardly understood at home—that Pictet, the head of the University at Geneva, translated my theory of the Natural Bridge into French, maintaining it to be the only scientific solution. Terrell said all the learned there spoke in recommendation of it. . . ."

From the above we see that the man was being recognized as successful. His library on general jurisprudence was the best in the state, if not in the whole country, for Ticknor and Terrell had purchased many rare books for him abroad. Strangers as they passed through Baltimore and Washington saw Mr. Wirt and brought letters of introduction from him to Gilmer. Even in Winchester we catch sight of distinguished visitors, such as General Bernard,[1] Napoleon's aide, who gave them vivid descriptions of Waterloo, Dr. Wistar of Philadelphia, and the Abbé. From this last companion Gilmer had now to part, and from the letter I am about to give we see how dear his Virginia friends had been to the rare old man.

FRANK W. GILMER, ESQ.

NEW YORK, *9th November,* 1820.

Dear Sir and Friend,

Tomorrow in the Albion packet i sail for England, and from thence in January i will sail for Brazil, where i will be in the beginning of March. It is impossible to me to leave this continent without once more turning my eyes to Virginia, to you and Monticello. I leave you my representative in that State, and near the persons who attach me to it, and i doubt not of your acceptance of this charge. Mr. Jefferson, Col. Randolph and his excellent Lady and family, the family i am

---

[1] General Simon Bernard (1779-1839)—he seems to have revisited America with Lafayette in 1824.

the most attached to in all America, will receive my adieus from you. Do not forget also that pure and virtuous soul at Montpellier and his Lady. You will i hope live long, my dear friend, and you will every day more and more see with your eyes *what difference exists between the two philosophical Presidents, and the whole future contingent series of chiefs of your nation.*[1] You know the rest of my acquaintances in your noble State, and the degrees of consideration i have for each, and you will distribute my souvenirs in proportion. . . . . [He next mentions his election to the Albemarle Agricultural Society and requests Gilmer to return his thanks.]

Glory yourself in being a Virginian, and remember all my discourses about them. It is the lot i would have wished for me if i was a North American, being a South American i am glad to be a Brazilian and you shall hear of what i do for my country if i live.

Cras ingens iterabimus aquor—but every where, you will find me constantly and steadily

Your faithful and sincere friend

JOSEPH CORRÈA DE SERRA.

Corrèa did not go to Brazil. The altered condition of Portugal, due to the uprising of 1820, drew him back to his native country, and he became minister of finance under the constitutional government. He died in 1823, after as useful and as varied a life as it is given a man to lead.

But this chapter has already exceeded the limits intended for it, so I shall only mention one other incident and then bring it to a close. On the 25th of October, 1823, Gilmer sent Mr. Jefferson, with his compliments, the six books of Cicero's *De Re Publica*, which had been discovered by the celebrated Italian philologist, Angelo Mai, and published by him in 1822. I had known from his letters that Gilmer was

---

[1] It is proper to say that the italics are my own.

fond of the classics and especially of Cicero ; but I was some-what surprised to find that he kept up with European learning as assiduously as this fact would indicate.

In answer to this very letter, it would seem, came the important communication from Mr. Jefferson referred to at the close of the first chapter.

CHAPTER III.

THE LAW PROFESSORSHIP.

The letter of November 23d, 1823, in which Mr. Jefferson asked his young friend to act as commissioner for procuring professors from England has not been preserved; but we have Gilmer's answer of December 3d, which lets us see that something beside the new commission had been offered him. It has already been shown how important the professorship of law was in Mr. Jefferson's eyes; and we can form some idea of his estimate of Mr. Gilmer's abilities, when we learn that it was now proposed to entrust the chair to him. It would be useless to attempt to describe the young man's gratification: he knew full well what store the philosopher set by this particular chair, and to be so honored at the early age of thirty-three proved even to his naturally despondent nature that his life had not been in vain. But soon the flush of pride passed off, and serious questions began to propose themselves. He had an aptitude for speaking and for public life. He might reasonably look forward to Congress, and Virginians had been known to mount higher. Then the University was as yet *in posse* merely. The men who were to be his colleagues had not been secured; and, though he himself was to choose them, he did not know whether good men were available at the salaries offered. He had succeeded well at the bar and had long formed plans of retirement with moderate wealth and of devotion to some single theme that should give him an acknowledged position among men of letters. At a new university he would have a constant round of lectures to give,

48

which would leave little time for outside literary work ; and
the prospect of retirement with a fortune would be forever
banished from his view.   Then, too, he would be bound to
continuous duty, with a constitution far from strong and liable
to give way at any time.   All these considerations weighed
well with him, and we accordingly find him requesting time
for his decision.   But the commission was quite another thing,
which he could take in place of his usual trip to the Springs.
He had long desired to visit England and now he could go
under the best auspices.   And so we find him gladly accepting the charge and making some practical suggestions which
seem to have been acted on.   One of these was that the powers
of the agent should not be limited to Great Britain and Ire-
land, but should be extended to the continent where English
letters were beginning to be studied.[1]   Mr. Jefferson seems to
have removed all absolute restrictions on his agent's movements ; but his preference remained decidedly for England,
on account of the difficulties a European would have in
thoroughly mastering our language and in appreciating our
customs.

The proposal that Gilmer should accept the office of agent
to England seems to have been made him by three of the
board of visitors without Mr. Jefferson's knowledge.   Perhaps the law chair was held up before his eyes by his great
friend, Chapman Johnson, although it was well known that
Mr. Jefferson would have the deciding voice in that matter.
Even as late as January, 1824, Cabell and Cocke seemed to
have had no notion that Gilmer was in Mr. Jefferson's mind,
as may be seen from the following extract taken from a letter
of Cabell's, bearing date the 29th of January, 1824 :

"Gen. Cocke and myself have long been thinking of Chancellor Carr as the Law Professor ; and we would be happy if
there could be no commitment on that question.   Mr. Carr's
happy temper and manners, and dignified character, to say

---

[1] Madison's Writings, III, 353.

nothing of his talents and acquirements, induced us to think
of him as the head of the institution." [1]

Although the request that no commitment should be made,
might at first blush indicate a suspicion that Mr. Jefferson
had some one else in his mind, I do not think that such a
suspicion existed, for all of the board regarded Mr. Jefferson
as the father of the University, and their own votes as merely
marks of honorable confidence in him. I can discover no
trace of any self-seeking spirit, certainly not in Cabell or
Cocke.[2]

To this letter of Mr. Cabell's, Jefferson made the following
answer :

MONTICELLO, *February* 23, 1824.

* * *

I remark what you say on the subject of committing ourselves to any one for the Law appointment. Your caution is
perfectly just. I hope, and am certain, that this will be the
standing law of discretion and duty with every member of
our Board in this and all cases. You know that we have all,
from the beginning, considered the high qualifications of our
professors as the only means by which we could give to our
institution splendor and pre-eminence over all its sister seminaries. The only question, therefore, we can ever ask ourselves, as to any candidate, will be, is he the most highly
qualified? The College of ——— has lost its character of
primacy by indulging motives of favoritism and nepotism,
and by conferring appointments as if the professorships were
intrusted to them as provisions for their friends. And even
that of Edinburgh, you know, is also much lowered from the
same cause. We are next to observe, that a man is not quali-

[1] Jefferson-Cabell Correspondence, page 289.
[2] But Mr. Madison was acquainted with Mr. Jefferson's purpose, and had
from the beginning preferred Gilmer to any of the learned lawyers proposed for the chair, as appears from a letter of his to Jefferson, Nov. 11,
1823. See Madison's Writings, III, 343.

fied for a professor, knowing nothing but merely his own profession. He should be otherwise well educated as to the sciences generally; able to converse understandingly with the scientific men with whom he is associated, and to assist in the councils of the Faculty on any subject of science on which they may have occasion to deliberate. Without this, he will incur their contempt and bring disreputation on the institu-tion.) With respect to the professorship you mention, I scarcely know any of our judges personally; but I will name, for example, the late Judge ——— who, I believe, was generally admitted to be among the ablest of them. His knowledge was confined to the common law merely, which does not constitute one-half the qualification of a really learned lawyer, much less that of a Professor of Law for an University. And as to any other branches of science, he must have stood mute in the presence of his literary associates, or of any learned strangers or others visiting the University. Would this constitute the splendid stand we propose to take?[1]

The individual named in your letter is one of the best, and to me the dearest of living men. From the death of his father, my most cherished friend, leaving him an infant in the arms of my sister, I have ever looked on him as a son. Yet these are considerations which can never enter into the question of his qualifications as a Professor of the University. Suppose all the chairs filled in similar degree, would that present the object which we have proposed to ourselves, and promised to the liberalities and expectations of our country? In the course of the trusts which I have exercised through life, with powers of appointment, I can say with truth, and unspeakable comfort, that I never did appoint a relation to office, and that merely because I never saw the case in which some one did not offer or occur, better qualified; and I have the most unlimited confidence that in the appointment of

---

[1] What would Jefferson say to the specialists now forming our modern faculties?

Professors to our nursling institution, every individual of my
associates will look with a single eye to the sublimation of
its character, and adopt as our sacred motto, 'detur digniori.'
In this way it will honor us, and bless our country. . . ."[1]

It is evident, I think, from the stress laid upon general
scientific and literary attainments, that the old diplomat
was trying to suggest Gilmer's appointment without being
obliged to mention his name or the fact that he had long ago
made up his own mind and consulted Gilmer about it.

Be this as it may, Carr's name was taken out of the list of
possible appointees by his being elected a judge of the Court
of Appeals—a position which his friends had long desired for
him, and which he had, doubtless, dreamed about himself.
There is a good deal of correspondence about this matter contained in the two volumes before me, and I subjoin a letter
from Francis Gilmer to Carr announcing the latter's election.
This letter will give a fair sample of the familiar intercourse
between Wirt and Carr, and the two Gilmers—Peachy and
Francis. I may remark that the office had long been depend-
ing upon the death of a once respectable but now super-
annuated judge, and that some of the letters on the subject
remind one strikingly of the magnificent chapter with which
" Barchester Towers " begins.

Conference room Ct. Appeals
24th *Feby.* 1824

To the honorable Dabney Carr Puisne Judge of the Court
of Appeals. It grieveth my heart most noble judge, that in
the five years I have lived here, I have been able to do no
more for thee, than sound thy praises, for this office, which
long due has come at last— Thy merit hath won it, & not
the feeble efforts of thy friends. The ballot was thus to-day
½ pas[t] 2 o'clock.

---

[1] Jefferson-Cabell Correspondence, page 391. Quoted also by Randall,
III, 497.

1st Ballot	Carr	90.	Barbour[1] 66.	Brock[o.2] 39.
2nd ——	Carr 114.	Barbour	87
Come down as soon as you can.

Your friend,

F. W. GILMER.

It was equally a matter of gratification to Gilmer that Henry St. G. Tucker was chosen to succeed Carr as chancellor of the Winchester district. Thus was fulfilled that remarkable prophecy mentioned by Kennedy in his life of Wirt. Wirt had long ago been made Attorney General, James Barbour had been sent to the Senate and was soon to be Secretary of War, and Dabney Carr was judge of the Court of Appeals.[3]

It had been resolved to keep Gilmer's mission a secret, for fear that American patriotism would howl down the newly-built walls of the University as soon as it was known that British voices would be heard therein. Few letters were written about it, but they show incidentally that the young agent went up to Albemarle early in the spring of 1824 and there held many consultations with his chief, in which Mr. Madison of course shared. But even then the newspapers got some inkling of what was going on, and we find in the Richmond *Enquirer* for May 18th, 1824, the following item in very small type: " Mr. F. W. Gilmer of this city has sailed for England, it is said, to make arrangements (for library, apparatus, &c.) to put the University of Virginia into immediate operation." It was then deemed best to put a bold face on

---

[1] P. P. Barbour of Orange County, previously Speaker of the House of Representatives, afterwards Associate Justice of the Supreme Court of the United States.

[2] Wm. Brockenborough, then a judge of the General Court. In ten years he took·his seat beside Carr as a judge of the Court of Appeals.

[3] In one of their trips to the Fluvanna court, James Barbour began taking off the peculiarities of his companions and wound up by predicting that they would rise to the offices mentioned in the text. See Kennedy's Life of Wirt, I, 71.

the matter and to enter into explanations. Accordingly in the same newspaper for May 25th, Gen. Cocke gave a notice of the progress of the University, in which he stated that an agent had gone to England for professors, but laid great stress on the fact that the chairs of government and morals had been reserved for native Americans.

In the meantime, however, Mr. Gilmer had hurried through Washington "incog," as he expressed it to Mr. Wirt, and, arriving in New York, had sailed early on the morning of May the 8th on the packet Cortes, bound for Liverpool.

I shall end this chapter by requesting the reader to imagine him pacing the deck and laughing at sea-sickness, longing to catch sight of the English shore and wondering whether the reality would equal his dreams—also perhaps glancing over his papers, among which lay letters of introduction from both Madison and Jefferson[1] to Richard Rush, our Minister at London.[2]

---

[1] These letters are to be found in Madison's Writings, III, 437, and Randall's Life of Jefferson, III, 497.

In Jefferson's letter Gilmer is mentioned as "the best educated subject we have raised since the Revolution; highly qualified in all the important branches of science, professing particularly that of the Law, which he has practised some years at our Supreme Court with good success and flattering prospects." Jefferson goes on to say that he does not expect to get such men as Cullen and Robertson and Porson, but he hopes to get the men who are treading on their heels, and who may prefer certain success in America to uncertain success in England.

[2] This gentleman (1780–1859) was a son of the well known Dr. Benjamin Rush and filled the offices of Attorney General of the United States, of temporary Secretary of State, of Minister to England (1817–25), of Secretary of the Treasury under John Quincy Adams, and Minister to France. He was also the author of " Memoranda of a Resident at the Court of St. James," &c. The edition of 1845 does not mention Gilmer's visit.

CHAPTER IV.

THE MISSION.

On Sunday, the 6th of June, 1824, Mr. Gilmer found himself in Liverpool. His first task was to write to Mr. Jefferson of his safe arrival. We may imagine the pleasure it gave the old gentleman to receive this short epistle on the 29th of July, and to sit in his library with the precious missive in his hands indulging pleasant day-dreams about the child of his old age. Professors and a library were now all he wanted and for these he depended on Gilmer alone; for his own life was evidently drawing to a close, and if anything happened to this agent, he might not live to see his University opened and to say his *"nunc dimittis."* The letter was, as I have said, a short one. The ship had been twenty-six days making from New York to Holyhead. For six days they had been driven about by adverse gales in St. George's channel, and Gilmer had in despair disembarked at Holyhead and gone through Wales to Liverpool. He went to Liverpool instead of London for business purposes which the letter does not explain.

The next communication with Mr. Jefferson is from London and bears the date of June 21st. I shall now let Mr. Gilmer tell his own story, only adding such facts and explanations as seem to be important.[1]

---

[1] In the letters which follow I have not consciously made any alterations except occasionally in punctuation and in substituting full for abbreviated forms.

LONDON, 21*st June*, 1824.

Dear Sir.

I wrote to you at Liverpool informing you of my arrival on the sixth. Hatton lying immediately in my way to London, I determined to call on Dr. Parr; unluckily for me, he had gone to Shrewsbury, and I shall be obliged to visit Hatton again, before I go to Oxford.

Since my arrival in London eight days ago, Mr. Rush (who is soon to return to the U. S.) has been so constantly engaged, that he could do nothing for me till yesterday. Indeed, the persons with whom he was to act, have been equally occupied in Parliament, the session being near its close, and as with us, the business of weeks is crowded into the few last days. Yesterday (Sunday) I received the necessary letters to Cambridge, Oxford, and Edinburgh, from Lord Teignmouth[1] and Mr. Brougham, Sir James Mackintosh being so occupied with the London and Manchester petitions for the recognition of the Independence of S. America that he has done nothing for us. I have conversed both with Lord T. and Mr. Brougham, who have both taken a lively interest in the object of my mission; the latter especially is very ardent for our success.

Finding no specific objection, nor indeed any objection, to Dr. Blaetterman[n], I have closed the engagement with him, as I considered myself instructed to do. He will sustain a considerable loss by his removal, having recently taken and furnished a large house. I did not therefore hesitate to offer him in the outset $1500 for the first year, with an intimation that he would probably be reduced to $1000 in the second, but leaving that entirely to the Visitors, preferring to make positive stipulations for the shortest possible time. Nor did I hint even anything of the guarantee of $2500.

Having thus concluded my arrangements in London, I shall set out to-morrow for Cambridge, where my real difficulties

---

[1] John Shore—Lord Teignmouth (1751–1834)—was an Indian official of some distinction, but is best known as the Editor of Sir Wm. Jones' works.

will begin, and where they will be greatest. I have anticipated all along that it would be most difficult to procure a fit
mathematician and experimental philosopher; for both are in
great demand in Europe. Mr. Brougham intimated that it
was by no means improbable, that Ivory[1] (the first mathematician without rival in G. B.) might be induced to engage for
us: and I should certainly have gone at once to Woolwich to
see him; but he accompanied the statement by remarking that
he had recently been a good deal disordered in his mind and
unable to attend to his studies. He had recovered, but there
is always danger of a recurrence of these maladies. Say nothing of this, however; for I may find this account exaggerated,
or wholly untrue, and may hereafter confer with Ivory, and
possibly contract with him.

I can do nothing about the books and apparatus till I have
engaged professors; all that part of my undertaking is therefore deferred until my return to London. I have seen Lack-
ington's[2] successors, and endeavoured to impress upon them
the importance of attention and moderate charges in their
dealings with us.

You will hear from me again from Cambridge; accept
therefore I pray you my best wishes.

P. S. Blaetterman[n] is in the prime of life—has a wife
and two small children, and they appear amiable and domes-
tic:[3] he speaks English well, tho' not without a foreign accent;

---

[1] James Ivory (1765–1842) was educated at the University of St.
Andrews, and, after studying theology and drifting from teaching to super-
intending a flax spinning factory, was, in consequence of his remarkable
memoirs on mathematical subjects, appointed professor of that study in
the Royal Military Academy at Marlow. This Gilmer mistook for Woolwich, and consequently he never found Ivory, who had resigned his professorship in 1819. Brougham continued to be Ivory's friend, for in 1831
he got him a pension of £300. See Gentleman's Mag., May, 1843, p. 537.

[2] Booksellers recommended by Mr. Jefferson.

[3] I could not help smiling on reading this ingenuous remark, for I
remembered to have heard that Dr. B. was afterwards dismissed from the
University for beating his wife. I do not know whether this report was

that we are obliged to encounter every way, as there are no profound English professors of modern language[s].

It appears from this letter, and from the letter of introduction to Rush, that Mr. Jefferson already knew of Dr. George Blaettermann, and that Gilmer went prepared to engage him, if possible, as professor of modern languages. Of Dr. Blaettermann's antecedents I have been unable to procure any information. Recommendations of the man appear to have been sent to Jefferson by George Ticknor as early as 1819.

Although Mr. Rush was very busy, he managed to find time to write Gilmer a long letter on the 16th of June in which he states that he had written to the three distinguished men mentioned in the letter just given, and that although Mr. Jefferson had overrated his ability to be of use to Mr. Gilmer, his disposition to be so used could not be overrated. Lord Teignmouth in replying to Mr. Rush on the date last mentioned enclosed four letters of recommendation, to two representative men at Oxford and Cambridge respectively. Three of these letters were written by his son in their joint names, the fourth was addressed by Lord Teignmouth himself to Dr. Coplestone (whose name he misspells) at Oxford. His lordship's courteous note hardly needs to be inserted. Dr. Edward Coplestone (1776–1849), afterwards Bishop of Llandaff and one of the first English clergymen to learn Welsh that his congregation might understand him, was at this time Provost of Oriel. Gilmer could not have been referred to a better man; but as the letter in which he describes his visit to Oxford, does not mention Dr. Coplestone, it is possible that the two did not meet. Coplestone could have given him excellent advice as to his selection of a classical professor; for he had himself

---

true, but it bears a curious relation to the story told about his successor, another foreigner, who was forced to leave because his wife beat *him*.

defended elegant classical scholarship against the Edinburgh reviewers.[1]

Brougham's note to Mr. Rush I give in full.

HILL ST., *Saturday.*

My dear Sir—

I am extremely sorry that I have not been able sooner to answer your very interesting letter—inclosing one from your truly venerable friend—I feel the liveliest interest in the success of Mr. G's mission—which is of great importance to both countries—but the difficulty is not small which Mr. Jefferson most sagaciously points out. I have inclosed three letters to the fittest persons at Cambridge & Edinburgh. At the latter place I am quite sure, he ought to say nothing to any one—but quietly go to Mr. Murray[2]—who intimately knows all the learned men there—& in whose judgement and honour he may safely trust. As for Cambridge, Dr. Davy[3]—the master of Caius College to whom I give him a letter, is now in London & will be here for two days longer—I shall see him to-morrow & consult him generally upon the subject—& if Mr. G. could be kind enough to call here to-morrow morning soon after eleven, I could take him to the Dr.—and I should beside, be

---

[1] I must once for all acknowledge my indebtedness to Mr. Leslie Stephen's wonderful Dictionary of National Biography. I have drawn from it whenever I could. Appleton's Cyclopædia of American Biography and Drake's American Biography have also been of service to me. I have indicated other sources of information where they seemed important.

[2] Undoubtedly Mr. John A. Murray, the eminent Whig lawyer, co-editor at one time of the Edinburgh Review, Clerk of the Pipe (a sinecure which got him a slap from Christopher North in the *Noctes*) and afterwards a Scotch Justice. Lord Murray's hospitality is amply testified to. It will be seen that he was very kind to Gilmer. (See Mrs. Gordon's "Christopher North," New York, 1875, page 387.)

[3] Dr. Martin Davy (1763–1839) was a successful physician who was made Master of Caius in 1803. In spite of some questionable proceedings, he is considered to have been a good master upon the whole. He was a strong Whig and a great friend of Dr. Parr's.

desirous of seeing him & putting him on his guard against
the various deceptions or rather *exaggerations* which will be
practised upon him—if he lets the object of his mission be
known to any but a very few.

Believe me to be,

Wt. great respect

and esteem

Your faithful Serv't

H. BROUGHAM.

From the execrable hand and the constant abbreviations to
be seen in this note one might infer, even if one did not know
it already, that Mr. Brougham was then the busiest man in
London.

In the meantime Mr. Jefferson had written Gilmer a letter,
which though not received until later, may as well be inserted
here.

MONTICELLO, *June* 5, '24.

Dear Sir.

The printer having disappointed me in getting ready, in
time to send to you before your departure, the original report
of the plan of the University, I now inclose you half a dozen
copies, one for Dr. Stuart [he meant Dugald Stewart], the
others to be disposed of as you please. I am sorry to inform
you that we fail in getting the contingent donation of 50 M. D.
[$50,000] made to us by our last legislature. so we have
nothing more to buy books or apparatus. I cannot help
hoping however that the next session will feel an incumbency
on themselves to make it good otherwise. an easy mode may
occur. W^m and Mary college, reduced to 11 students, and to
the determination to shut their doors on the opening of ours,
are disposed to petition the next legislature to remove them to
Richmond. it is more reasonable to expect they will consoli-
date them with the University. this would add about 6 M. D.
a year to our revenue.

Soon after you left us, I received from Maj^r Cartwright, a
well-known character in England, a letter, and a volume on
the English constitution. having to answer his letter, I put
it under your cover, with a wish you could deliver it in person.
it will probably be acceptable to yourself to have some personal acquaintance with this veteran and virtuous patriot; and
it is possible he may be useful to you, as the favorable sentiments he expresses towards our University assure me he would
willingly be. perhaps he would accept a copy of the Report,
which I would ask you to present him in my name. ever &
affectionately yours

TH: JEFFERSON.

On the back of this is endorsed, "Received Cambridge,
14th July, 1824—without the pamphlets, so could not take
one to D. Stewart." But the reports seem to have come later.
Gilmer now left London for Cambridge from which place
he wrote the following letter to Mr. Jefferson :

CAMBRIDGE, 7th July, 1824.
Dear Sir,

I left London for this place on the 22d of June, immediately I had procured from Mr. Rush the necessary letters. I
found on my arrival here the same evening that the long
vacation at the University had virtually commenced three
weeks before, that is while I was at sea. Of the three persons
to whom I had letters, he, on whom Mr. Brougham principally relied, was absent on a visit of a week.[1] I employed
the time as well as I could, in enquiring into the state of
learning here, and what in this dilemma would be my best
method of proceeding. I found natural history very little
attended to, and should therefore be content to procure a
Mathematician and Natural Philosopher from this University,
indeed from what I can learn, there are no particular reasons
for preferring the Professor of experimental philosophy from

[1] Dr. Davy.

Cambridge. But they from whom I should have had some chance of selecting fit persons, had, in all the departments of learning, gone to their various homes in different parts of the kingdom. This puts me in some respects to great disadvantage, for I shall have to travel a vast deal to see them. As yet I have learned but of one, whom I should probably choose, that is a Mr. Atkinson,[1] formerly "Wrangler" in Trinity College, Cambridge, now teaching a school in Scotland. He is spoken of as a first rate mathematician, and I shall endeavor to see him in my visit to Scotland.

For the teacher of ancient languages two have been suggested, both residing in London. I defer acting on that branch, until I visit Oxford and see Dr. Parr. Sir James Edw. Smith is at the head of natural history in England, and he was in Norfolk when I was in London—as he is now. Being nearer him than I shall be again in my regular route, I shall spend part of a day with him, proceed to Oxford, and then to Edinburgh. It seemed to be thought most probable that our Professor of natural history will be best found in Scotland, or at London, tho' we shall any where find it difficult to procure one learned both in botany and zoology. From what I hear our Professor of medicine shall probably come also from London, but I shall form no opinion of this, until I see Edinburgh. After remaining sometime at Oxford and Edinburgh, I shall return to London, as a central point, and make short excursions as I may find necessary, in order to complete the important object of my mission. I shall forbear to give any general opinion until I have seen Oxford and Edinburgh.

The manner of my reception at Cambridge has softened my profound respect and veneration for the most renowned

---

[1] Henry Atkinson (1781–1829) of Newcastle on Tyne is the only Atkinson of mathematical celebrity that I can discover. He did teach in Scotland; but he does not appear ever to have been at Cambridge; for at the age of thirteen he was principal of a school !

University in the world into a warm esteem for all connected
with it. From the Bishop of Bristol[1] and Dr. Davy down
to the undergraduates, all have vied with each other in the
profusion and delicacy of their civilities. I have dined more
than half the days in the Hall of Trinity College, the most
famous of all, and was delighted with the urbanity and good
breeding of the fellows, students and of every one who
appeared. The tone of feeling in England is undoubtedly
favorable to us of the U. S. I have heard every where the
warmest expressions of friendship for us, and have certainly
received. every civility possible. At the great festival at the
College yesterday, every one with whom I conversed enquired
with the utmost earnestness into the different departments of
our affairs; the Lawyers are beginning to read our reports,
the courts and even the Parliament have in several things followed, and somewhat boastfully, I may say, our example. I
am very glad of all this; for now we have grown beyond the
reach of this enormous creature, at once a Leviathan and a
Lion, there is no good in keeping alive angry feelings.

Mr. Brougham enquired about you with the greatest interest. I shall write you again from Oxford, &c.

I do not know whether the proposed visit was made to Sir
James Edward Smith. If Gilmer did not see the latter gentleman, then within four years of his death, we may be sure
that he relinquished the visit with disappointment, for Sir
James was the most distinguished botanist in England, having
been the founder of the Linnæan Society, and botany had
always been Gilmer's favorite study. We shall see hereafter
that this trip to Cambridge was successful in more than a
social sense, for by it Gilmer was enabled to secure two of the
best of the first professors.

---

[1] Dr. J. Kaye (1783–1853) had become Bishop of Bristol on the death of
Dr. Mausel in 1820. He had been Master of Christ's College and Regius
Professor of Divinity. I may remark that Dr. Christopher Wordsworth
was at this time Master of Trinity.

The promised letter from Oxford does not seem to have been written, but in the meantime we have two letters of a more personal nature which seem worthy of presentation and require no comments.

The first is to his brother, Peachy Gilmer, and I deem it proper to say that I have not had time to verify any of Gilmer's statements, except such as are germane to the subject of this essay.

BOSTON, 2 *July*, 1824.
(Lincolnshire.)

My dear brother,

This is the place our Boston of Massachusetts was called after. The daughter has outgrown the mother. This is a very small town, on a very small stream, what we would call a creek, here dignified with the name of river, with very small trade, and in short with nothing large about it, except a most enormous tower to the church, which I came here principally to see. For when I got to Cambridge, I found one of the principal persons I was to consult with, absent for some days, and not to lose the time, I took a small circuit to Peterborough, Lincoln, and Boston, passing in my way thro' Stilton, famous for chesees, a village not as large as Liberty.[1]

Lincoln is of great antiquity, and has one of the finest Cathedrals in England. The site of it (the Cathedral) too is beautiful—it stands on an eminence higher and more abrupt than the capitol hill of Richmond—all around is one vast plain, till lately a fen, reclaimed and now a lovely meadow. The town of Lincoln is no great matter; here, too, is a tower of W^m. the Conqueror,—a palace of John of Gaunt, a Roman court, with chequered pavement, &c. From Lincoln I descended the Witham to this place. The Witham is about as large as the canal near the basin; it flows thro' an unbroken meadow, not of great fertility, nor at all beautiful, or pictur-

---

[1] Peachy Gilmer lived for some years at Liberty, a small town in Bedford county, Va.

esque, tho' you see steeples and towers on all sides. The
country of Lincoln is richer in old buildings than any part
of England, but the country was by nature, I think, not
generally fertile, something like those cold, iron-ore bogs we
sometimes have, black and of rich appearance, but of no life
or strength.

My reception at Cambridge was what has given me most
pleasure. . . . . I have been really domesticated (& was
invited to take rooms) in Trinity College, the most renowned
without doubt in the world. It is the favorite College of the
nobility and gentry of England—here were educated Bacon,
Coke, Harvey, Newton, Cotes, Cowley, Dryden, &c. &c.
They shewed MS. letters of Newton, and several of the inter-
lined originals of Milton's smaller Poems, part of his original
Paradise Lost, &c. &c., and at Christ's College (which was
Milton's) the Bishop of Bristol shewed me the mulberry tree
Milton planted ; a fine bust of him, and many curious things
else. I walked moreover to Granchester, (2 miles from Cambridge) supposed to be the country church yard, Gray had in
mind, in his immortal elegy. It was ever a favorite walk
with Gray, lying thro' hedges, covered with wild roses and
briars, a meadow on the margin of the Cam—I heard "the
Curfew toll the knell of parting day" at 9 o'clock. But all
this did not give one-half the pleasure I have derived a
thousand times from repeating the elegy, in hours of "lonely
contemplation," which heaven has given me in kindness or in
wrath, God knows which. I go to-morrow to Cambridge,
thence to Oxford, thence to Edinburgh.

The eastern side of England is not beautiful, and with all
those noble steeples and towers, but for Cambridge, I should
have found small pleasure since I left London. The country
west of London was every where (except Staffordshire) most
enchanting ; tho' by nature rather less fertile, I think, than I
have heard it represented. I was at the House of Commons,
the Courts, Westminster Abbey, (which has nothing but Henry
VII's Chapel and its awful history to interest me) and every

where, but I hate descriptive writing and descriptive reading, but not descriptive talking, so I will give you the whole when we meet.

I saw J. Randolph in London—looking badly. You will think it strange, fondly treated as I was at Cambridge, that I should think of returning. I assure you I already begin to languish for Virginia. I never liked being jostled from place to place—crowds or strangers—here are all. Since I left London, I have not seen a single person. I have found John Bull far more civil every where than he is represented to be. The tone of manners in the higher walks, is exactly what I have seen in Virginia. McClurg, John Walker, old Mr. Fleming[1] &c. were fully as elegant as Lord Teignmouth or Lord Bishop of Bristol &c. but not more so, for the manners of all were unexceptionable. There is less dashing than you suppose, less pretension than with the *new-born gentility* of the Eastern States.

I do not know when I may have leisure to write again. I am detained a day here for a coach, and calling you all to mind & heart, I could not resist the temptation of addressing a few words to you. . . . . .

The next is to Mr. Wirt and has been taken from Kennedy's Life (Vol. II, 187.)

July 16, 1824.

My dear Mr. Wirt,

I write you my first letter from England, not from Warwick Castle or Guy's Cliff,—which are both near at hand—nor from Stratford generally, but from the identical room in which the immortal bard first came "into this breathing

---

[1] Fleming was, possibly, the judge whom Dabney Carr succeeded. Walker I do not know of—unless he was the John Walker who was appointed to succeed Grayson in the Senate in 1790. As I cannot ascertain the date of this Walker's death, the point must remain in doubt, but from an expression used in another letter I am inclined to think that he was the man.

world." Here day first dawned upon his infant eyes—a miserable hovel. Imagine in that hovel a small room, with a low roof; but one window,—that looking to the setting sun; a fire-place advanced into the room, by the naked chimney coming through the floor. The house is neither wood nor brick, but a wooden frame with the intervals filled up with brick. The wooden beams are shrunk and warped by weather and time. On the lower floor is a butcher's stall. Nowhere is there a single vestige of Shakespeare. His chair is gone. His mulberry tree, which was in the garden, is attached to another house; it is reduced to the last fibre. Except his will, and the walls and beams of this lowly mansion, I know of no object in existence which he touched. Here the wise and the great repair to worship him. In the register before me is the name of Sir Walter Scott among other less illustrious. The walls were once scribbled over by men of genius and fame—Fox, Pitt, and others,—but a mischievous tenant lately whitewashed them, and you see only what have been recently written.

His body lies near the altar in the church, and neither name, nor date, nor arms appear upon the stone; conclusive circumstances, I think, to show that he wrote the epitaph which is sculptured upon the stone. This has been doubted. What but the modesty of his own great mind could limit the epitaph of Shakespeare to the expression of the simple wish that his bones might rest undisturbed in their last repository? We have seen the lines in Johnson's life of him, but here is a *fac simile:*[1]

I inquired of half a dozen persons in Stratford for the tomb of Shakespeare before I could find it. I should not have been surprised if this had occurred in a search for the tomb of Newton or Milton. But I was amazed at its happening in the case of the poet of all ages and conditions.

.   .   .   .

---

[1] Here follow the well-known lines.

I begin to be impatient to see Virginia once more. It is more like England than any other part of the United States—slavery *non obstante.* Remove that stain, blacker than the Ethiopian's skin, and annihilate our political schemers, and it would be the fairest realm on which the sun ever shone. I like the elbow room we have, where the wild deer cross the untrodden grass, and the original forest never heard the echo of the woodman's axe. There is nothing in England so beautiful as the scenery of Albemarle, or the view from Montevideo—the window from which you used to gaze on the deep blue depth of these [those?] silent and boundless mountains.

Peace to them!—and a blessing warm, though from afar, on you and all your house!

Yours affectionately,

F. W. Gilmer.

Having tarried some days in Oxford, Gilmer went to pay his respects to Dr. Parr, to whom Mr. Jefferson had given him a letter and from whom he expected much assistance in his choice of a classical professor. Nearly everyone has heard of Dr. Parr, scarcely anyone has read a line of what he wrote. He was now in his seventy-seventh year, and, we may not doubt, wore his wig as of old, smoked shag tobacco, and talked about how narrowly he escaped being made a bishop. But to the reader of De Quincey and of the *Noctes Ambrosianae* any description I can give of this quaint old scholar, who certainly knew more Latin than any man living, will seem lame and borrowed; so, presuming that my readers have read the *Noctes,* I shall merely remark that Gilmer called upon him on the 17th of July, but found him setting out "on his travels," which proved not extensive as he sent Gilmer a note inviting him to come back the next morning. The handwriting in this note is only equalled by that of the celebrated Du Pont. Our next letter is to Mr. Jefferson, written from Dr. Parr's:

HATTON, *July 20th*, 1824.

Dear Sir.

Doctor Parr (Samuel) was delighted with your letter, and received me with the greatest kindness: I have now been two days with him. Tho' not above 76 years of age, I soon discovered that he was too infirm, to be of much service to us in the selection of professors. Tho' he is our decided and warm friend, my interview with him has been the most discouraging. He has however been of great service, by assisting me in forming a catalogue of classical Books for the university.

I found at Oxford as at Cambridge, that Professors and students, had all gone to their summer residence, and I could consequently make no inquiries at all there. I have now however, seen enough of England, and learned enough of the two universities, to see, that the difficulties we have to encounter, are greater even than we supposed; not so much from the variety of applications, as from the difficulty of inducing men of real abilities to accept our offer. By far the greater portion of any assembly so numerous as that which fills the walls of Oxford and Cambridge, must of course be composed of persons of very moderate capacity. Education at the Universities has become so expensive, that it is almost exclusively confined to the nobility and the opulent gentry, no one of whom could we expect to engage. Of the few persons at Oxford, or Cambridge, who have any extraordinary talent, I believe 99 out of 100, are designed for the profession of law, the gown, or aspire to political distinction; and it would be difficult to persuade one of these, even if poor, to repress so far the impulse of youthful ambition as to accept a professorship in a college in an unknown country. They who are less aspiring, who have learning, are caught up at an early period in their several colleges; soon become fellows, & hope to be masters, which with the apartments, garden, and 4. 5. or 600 £ sterling a year, comprises all they can imagine of comfort or happiness. Just at this time too, there are building at Cambridge, two very large colleges attached to Trinity, and King's, which will be the most splendid of all. This creates a new demand for professors, and raises new hopes in the graduates.

All these difficulties are multiplied by the system we have been compelled to adopt in accumulation [accumulating] so many burthens on one professor. To all the branches of natural philosophy, to add chemistry and astronomy, each of very great compass, strikes them here with amazement.

The unprecedented length of the session you propose, is also a dismaying circumstance. As this will probably be altered in time, it is, I think, to be regretted that we had not begun with longer vacations. At Cambridge and Oxford there are three vacations. The longest is from about the 1st July to the 10th October, altogether there is a holiday of near 5 months. I inquired at Cambridge if there was any good reason for this long recess. They answered, " It is indispensable : no one could study in such hot weather." . . . . "It is necessary to refresh the constitution, oppressed by the continued application of many months," &c. If the heat be insufferable in England, what must it be in our July, August, &c when there is to be no vacation ?

I see distinctly that it will be wholly impossible to procure professors *from either University,* by the time you wished. Whether I can find them elsewhere in England, is most doubtful ; in time I fear not. I shall not return without engaging them, if they are to be had, in G. B. or Germany. I have serious thoughts of trying Göttingen, where the late political persecutions of men of letters will naturally incline them to us and where classical literature, at least, is highly cultivated. Dr. Parr seems to prefer this course, but I shall not be hasty in adopting it, as I fear the want of our language will prove a great obstacle. [Here he makes some remarks about his personal expenses being greater than he had supposed and requests that the Board of Visitors forward another bill.]

I set out for Edinburgh to-morrow, shall remain there as long as I find any advantage to our object, in doing so, and

259]   English Culture in Virginia.   71

shall return to London. There I shall be able to learn whether
I had best go to Germany, seek English scholars in the
country, or quietly wait till the Universities open in October
which would delay any final contract till December or January.
I am not disheartened—at least we must keep things well, to
present a good front to the next legislature. That I shall do,
if possible.

I received your letter to Maj^r Cartwright while at Cambridge. I have not been to London since. &c.

Leaving Hatton on the 21st of July, Gilmer was in Edinburgh by the 25th, on which day he received a letter, in answer
to one of his own, from a young man he had met and taken a
fancy to in Cambridge. This was no other than Thomas
Hewett Key, first professor of mathematics in the University
of Virginia. Mr. Key was at this time in his 26th year and
a master of arts of Trinity College, Cambridge. For two
years past he had been applying himself to the study of
medicine, but Gilmer, having met him at the rooms of Mr.
Praed at Cambridge [evidently the exquisite society poet—
Winthrop Mackworth Praed] perceived his fine scientific
gifts and invited him by letter to become a member of the
faculty. Key's answer (written from London on the 23rd
of July) is now before me and runs as follows :

FRIDAY, July 23, 1824,
39 Lombard St., London.[1]

Dear Sir,

Let me first apologize to you for any delay I may appear
to have been guilty of in not sending a more early answer to

---

[1] The two letters from Key and Long which I have inserted may vary
slightly from the originals because they were intrusted to a stupid copyist
whose stupidity was not discovered until the MSS. volumes had passed out
of my possession. The variations are, I am certain, unimportant. All the
other letters were either copied directly by myself or had my personal
revision.

the letter I had the pleasure of receiving from you.   Not
finding me at Cambridge which I had left the same morning
with yourself, it was forwarded to my residence in town; and
as I took rather a circuitous route homewards, it was not till
two days after its arrival that it first came to my hands.

The first opportunity I had after the receipt of it, I communicated the contents to my Father under whose roof I am
living; and lost no time in consulting with him on the pro-
priety of accepting your proposal.   And before I say a word
more, you must allow me to thank you for the very handsome
and indeed too flattering manner in which that proposal has
been made to me.   And, while I express myself proud of the
favourable light in which you are pleased to view me, I assure
you that the feeling is at least reciprocal.   I had always the
utmost respect for your country ; and, believe me, that it has
been highly gratifying to me to find that opinion more than
justified by the first of her sons whom I have ever had the
pleasure to meet.   I have been now for two years applying
the greater part of my time to the study of medicine; and
had, reluctantly indeed, made the determination to withdraw
myself almost wholly from the pursuit of pure science and
literature.   Indeed nothing but your liberal proposition would
have induced me once more to turn my thoughts to that
quarter.   You will allow then that it is natural for one, who
has devoted so much of his time and no inconsiderable expense
to the study of an arduous profession, to pause ; and weigh
well every part of a proposal, which calls on him at once to
sacrifice all the progress he has made, and to embark again in
a perfectly new course.   And this caution is the more requisite
on the present occasion, since the mere distance would render
it difficult for me, in the case of disappointment, to retrace my
steps.   Of course in the short limits of a letter it is impossible
for either of us to say much ; and consequently in my present
imperfect acquaintance with the detail of your offer it must be
out of my power to come to any final arrangement till the
time when we meet in town, I will in the mean while state

generally what my feelings on the question are and leave you
to judge how far we are likely ultimately to coincide. I own
I have my share of ambition ; and every one who is not to be
numbered in the class of fools or rogues will confess as much ;
at the same time that ambition is of a character which is far
from inconsistent with promoting the happiness of others. I
have already said that I am fondly attached to the sciences ;
and the strength of that attachment is proportional to each, as
it appears to me calculated to advance the interests of man-
kind. In the university of Cambridge I have often thought
that this object is too much lost sight of ; and that the great
body of talent in that seat of knowledge is frequently directed
to points of comparatively minor importance, and thus in a
great measure thrown away whilst it might be employed in a
manner so highly beneficial both for England and the whole
world. It was a strong feeling of this kind, which, on the
last night I had the pleasure of meeting you, led me perhaps
to be too warm in the observations I made ; but I know not
whether such warmth was not justifiable. At any rate I had
the pleasure of knowing that what I then said had the effect
of directing the thoughts of one gentleman who was present
to my favorite subject of Political Economy ; and that gentlemen (I mean Mr. Drinkwater [1]) one whose talents I have
the highest respect for. Having these views of the real
objects of science, and actuated by an ambition which seeks,
as far as my poor means are able, to add to the sum total
of human happiness not merely in my own country but
generally, I shall be most happy, should I find it in my
power finally to agree to your offer. The manners, habits,
and sentiments of the country will of course be congenial
with my own ; and there can be little fear of my finding

---

[1] Mr. John Eliot Drinkwater-Bethune (1801–1851), son of the historian
of the Siege of Gibraltar, was afterwards counsel to the Home Office and
an Indian official of high standing. He is chiefly remembered in connection with his labors for the education of native girls of the higher castes.

myself unhappy in the society I am likely to meet with, considering the favourable specimen I have already seen. Nor would it at all grieve me in a Political point of view to become, if I may be allowed that honour, a Citizen of the United States. With all these prepossessions in favour of your proposal, it remains for me only to enquire into the particular nature of the appointment you have so kindly offered me. I would wait till you return to town for the explanations you have there promised ; but of course it must be unpleasant to both of us to remain in suspense, and you will look on it as not impertinent, but rather as a proof how eager I am to arrive at a final determination, if I put the following queries. 1$^{st.}$ What branch or branches of science you would wish me to devote my services to. 2$^{dly.}$ What duties I should have to perform; How far I should be at liberty to form my own plan of promoting that science; How far I should be under the direction of others and of whom; How far I should have the control of my own time. And if to this you could add an account of the existing state of the University, of its government, the average number, age, and pursuits of the students &c., you would do much to enable me to come to a decisive conclusion. It will of course be impossible to reply fully to these questions; and perhaps you can refer me to some person in town, to whom I may apply for immediate information ; which would be far preferable to the slow and necessarily confined channel of the Post Office. I trust too you will not think me guilty of any indelicacy if I ask how far the University has given you authority to make any private arrangement and whether any agreement between us will not require some form of ratification in Virginia. On reference to the maps I find that Charlottesville is the Capital of Albemarle county and that it is situated a considerable distance up the country. This of course must add much to the expense of my removal from this place to the University of Virginia and as this expense at the outset is a consideration of some importance to my empty purse I should be obliged to you if you could furnish me with an idea of it; and whether the University would be willing to diminish the weight of it. There are of course many other questions which on a little more reflection would suggest themselves to me; but I fear I have already drawn too largely on your time and patience. I will therefore conclude with assuring you that

I am, with the greatest consideration, your obliged servant,

THOMAS HEWETT KEY.

On the evening we met at Mr. Praed's, I remember to have offered you a letter to Mr. McCulloh,[1] who lately lectured in town on Political Economy. It did not then occur to me that Mr. M. is at this moment repeating his course at Liverpool, and that consequently you are not likely to meet with him at Edinburgh. I shall, of course, obey your wish that the communications between us should be held secret; and in consulting with my Father, you will perceive that I have violated only the letter of your request.

Gilmer answered this letter on the 26th, as follows:

EDINBURGH, *26th July*, 1824.

Dear Sir,

I have this morning received your letter of the 23d. and am gratified to find the temper of it just what I expected from you. I was aware that my proposition would require both time and examination into detail, and I therefore limited it to the general question in my former letter. I now take great pleasure in answering the enquiries you make, so far as the compass of a letter allows me; I shall with equal satisfaction enter into fuller explanations when I see you in London, which I hope will be about the middle of August.

---

[1] Mr. MacCulloch published his "Principles of Political Economy" about a year after this was written.

The Professorship which I supposed you would most willingly accept, as that for which your studies and predelections most eminently fitted you, is the chair of mathematics. We should require in the professor a competent knowledge of this science to teach it in all its branches to the full extent to which they have been explored and demonstrated in Europe—the differential calculus—its application to physics, the problem of the three bodies, &c., &c.

As to public utility. How can one be so useful in Europe, where the theatre in every department of science is more crowded with actors than with spectators, (if I may use the expression) as in the United States, where the mind of a great and rising nation is to be formed and , enlightened in the more difficult departments of learning? But to answer your interrogatories *seriatim,* I will first observe that I am armed with complete and full powers to make the contract final and obligatory at once, by a power of attorney, which you shall see.

Duties. Your office would be to teach the mathematical sciences by lessons, or lectures, whichever way you thought best, by a lecture on alternate days of an hour or hour and a half. And you will have nearly an absolute power as to the method of instruction. The only interference being by way of public examination, and the only thing required will be to find that the students make good progress.

Direction. The University of Virginia, by the statute of incorporation, (which I will show you) is under the management of seven visitors chosen by the Governor and Council of the State. The professors can be removed only by the concurring vote of $\frac{2}{3}$ of the whole number, *i. e.,* of 5 out of 7. These visitors are the most distinguished men, not of Virginia only, but of America, Mr. Jefferson, Mr. Madison, &c.

Time. Your time would be entirely at your own disposal, except that it would be expected you should derive no emolument from any other office, the duties of which were to be discharged by yourself personally.

Existing state of the University. The whole is now complete, ready for the reception of professors and of students. The houses for the professors are most beautiful; the great building for lectures, &c., is magnificent—being on the plan of the Pantheon in Rome.

Laws. The code of laws was not finished when I left Virginia; indeed, I believe it was purposely deferred, that my observations and those of the several professors might assist in the compilation. You may be assured they will be most liberal toward the professors.

Probable number of students. Mr. Jefferson told me he had inquiries almost every post from various parts of the United States, to know when they would open their doors. He thought the first year there would certainly be 500 pupils. Say that of these only 200 enter your course, and I should think nearly the whole would, and setting them down at 30 dolls. each, as the medium price, you would then receive from the students $6,000, from the university, $1,500 = to $7,500, or to £1,689 sterling. But if you received only £1,200 or £1,000, you would soon amass wealth enough to do as you pleased, for your expenses will not exceed £300 a year after the first year. You pay no rent for your house.

The University visitors are very desirous to open in February next. To assist you out, I shall be quite at liberty to pay you in advance enough to bear your expenses to Charlottesville, and your salary will do the business after your arrival. The passage is 30 guineas to Richmond, and it will not cost you 5 to reach Charlottesville, with all your *impedimenta.*

1. Now to another point. I wish to engage a first-rate scholar to teach the Latin and Greek languages profoundly— if he understand Hebrew, all the better.

2. A person capable of teaching anatomy and physiology thoroughly, with the history of the various theories of medicine, from Hippocrates down.

3. A person capable of demonstrating the modern system of physics, including astronomy.

4. A person capable of teaching natural history, including botany, zöology, mineralogy, chemistry, and geology.

You may probably be able to assist me in procuring fit persons for some of these departments, and you would do me a great favor. Could men of real learning and congenial habits be selected, it would make it one of the most pleasant situations that exist.

I should not omit to mention that Charlottesville is 80 miles above Richmond, the metropolis of the State, on navigable water, and already connected by the James River with Richmond.

Yours with great respect and consideration, &c.,

F. W. GILMER.

Five years will make you a citizen of the U. S., with a compliance with certain forms, about which I will direct you. Birth will make your posterity so—I wish them in anticipation, as I wish you most sincerely, a career of utility and of glory in our flourishing country.[1]

The next letter we have is one of August 1st, from Profes-

---

[1] This letter is taken from a first copy made by Mr. Gilmer. Through the kindness of Mr. Key's eldest daughter I was enabled to compare it with the final letter that was sent. The formal variations were considerable; but as the matter was practically the same, the differences are not noted. I wrote to George Long, Esquire, of Lincoln's Inn, to discover whether his father had left any papers or memoranda that bore upon the present study; but that gentleman was unable to furnish me with any data. In his courtesy, however, he communicated with Mr. Key's daughter, who was considerate enough to make the copy alluded to, for which I desire publicly to return my thanks. She recollects having heard her father speak of Gilmer in very pleasant terms. It will interest American readers to know that the two friends, Key and Long, whose intimacy began at Cambridge and continued through university life of fully fifty years, left families which, through intermarriage and friendship, seem likely to perpetuate the same pleasant relationship.

sor (afterwards Sir John) Leslie to Gilmer, at the Gibbs Hotel. Mr. Jefferson had thought that the great scientist, now Playfair's successor in the chair of natural philosophy, would be inimical to his pet institution. I suppose this was due to some misunderstanding that must have arisen when Leslie was in Virginia (1788–9) teaching in the Randolph family. It will be seen later that Mr. Jefferson labored under a misapprehension.

QUEEN STREET, *Sunday Evening.*

Dear Sir,

I stated to you that it appeared to me that even the temporary superintendence of a person of name from Europe might contribute to give eclat and consistency to your infant university. On reflecting since on this matter, I feel not averse, under certain circumstances, to offer my own services. I am prompted to engage in such a scheme partly from a wish to revisit some old friends, and partly from an ardent desire to promote the interests of learning and liberality. I could consent to leave Edinburgh for half a year. I could sail from Liverpool by the middle of April, visit the colleges in the New England States, New York and Philadelphia, spend a month or six weeks at Charlottesville. I should then bestow my whole thoughts in digesting the best plans of education, &c., give all the preliminary lectures in Mathematics, Natural Philosophy, and Chemistry, and besides, go through a course comprising all my original views and discoveries in Meteorology, Heat, and Electricity. Having put the great machine in motion, I should then take my leave to visit other parts of the Continent. But I should continue to exercise a parental care over the fortunes of our University, and urge forward the business by my correspondence, &c. To make such a sacrifice as this, however, I should expect a donation of at least one thousand pounds, which would include all my expenses on the voyage, &c. If you should think well of this proposition, you may consult your constituents. Were it acceded to, I should probably in the autumn visit both France and Germany, with the view of procuring aid and instruments to further our plans. But at all events, I trust you will not ment[ion] this c[onfi]dential communication w[hich] I send you on the spur of the moment. Whatever may be the decision, I shall at all times be ready to give you my sincere and impartial advice.

I ever am, Dear Sir,

Most truly yours,

JOHN LESLIE.

On the 7th of August, Gilmer wrote a letter to his friend, Chapman Johnson, a well-known lawyer in Richmond, and one of the Board of Visitors; but for some reason the letter was not sent. It touches on several interesting matters, and is therefore given here:

EDINBURGH, 7 *August,* 1825.

Dear Johnson,

I satisfied myself at the English Universities that it was idle to seek at either a professor in natural philosophy. They have no general lecturer on this important branch; but each college (where it is taught at all) has its own professor: none of them, I believe, equal to our old master, the bishop [Bishop Madison]. This department I found far more successfully cultivated in Scotland, and I looked to it or London as our only chance. Here I could learn of but one individual eminently qualified, and he being already engaged in a good business, I had no great hope of seducing him from Edinburgh. I have been a fortnight making inquiries and besetting him; he is to give a final answer this evening, [He did not for nearly a week] but I am impatient to be off to London, where as from a central point I can carry on two or three negotiations at once. If Buchanan (that is his name) accept my offer, I shall be well pleased. He is both practical and theoretical. He has written some learned articles in the supplement to the Encyclopedia Britannica, and is a matter-of-fact man, and equally qualified both for natural philosophy, properly [speaking], and for chemistry. And I now know by the fullest inquiry that what I told you is true—chemistry must be attached to natural philosophy, and astronomy to mathematics. You will hardly in all Europe find a good naturalist deep in chemistry, while every natural philosopher is pretty well acquainted with chemistry ; and few natural philosophers are deep in astronomy, while almost every mathematician is. So whether Buchanan and I agree or not, I have nearly given up the hope of uniting natural history and chemistry. [He then alludes to Leslie and Mr. Jefferson's fear that he would be hostile—accident had thrown them together, and they had become friends—Leslie having done more for him than anyone except Dr. Parr. He then cites Leslie's offer, and adds—] It seems to me, that as Leslie's name would give us immense renown, we should do a good deal to procure it. We might agree to give him so much and take the fees to ourselves, so as to get him there probably for less money than we will give another. The trustees should think of this, and if you come to any conclusion as to his offer, or as to getting him with us permanently, Mr. Jefferson may write to him, as if in a highly confidential manner. I know his letter will, at any rate, be well received, which Mr. J. does not believe.[1]

I think it a great pity your agent is so fettered by instructions. Your short vacation (6 weeks) has done immense mischief, and it cannot last a year. Think of 200 boys festering in one of those little rooms in August or July : the very idea is suffocating. You should have begun with three months, and gradually shortened it to two. If Buchanan and I disagree, it will be on this point only.

---

[1] Whether Leslie's offer was considered, or whether he withdrew it, I do not know. Gilmer's subsequent success would have ended the negotiation at any rate, had it been started ; but the fact that Leslie made such an offer is surprising.

It is time I should say something of the honor you designed
me.   Long as I have delayed it, I yet want the materials for
a final judgment, but think it proper to say that considering
the immense labors thrown on me, the very short vacation and
my prospects at the bar, a salary of $2,000 is the least I could
accept.   With that beginning in October to enable me to prepare my course in the winter, I believe I should accept it.
But not knowing that you will grant it on these terms, I think
it best to give you notice, that you may look elsewhere in
time.   If you would make me President or something, with
the privilege of residing anywhere within 3 miles of the Ro-
tunda, it would be a great inducement.   But to put me down
in one of those pavilions is to serve me as an apothecary
would a lizard or beetle in a phial of whiskey, set in a window
and corked tight.   I could not for $1,500 endure this, even if
I had no labor.

I have one of the finest men I saw at Cambridge in my eye
for mathematics.   I find him well disposed to us.   We are to
go into details when I return to London.

We shall find that the difficulties of combination here
alluded to were finally overcome, at least in the main.   Of the
correspondence between Gilmer and George Buchanan, only
two short notes from the latter have been preserved, one of
August 12th, the other of prior but uncertain date.   From
the second we learn that Buchanan wished a long vacation,
that he might revisit Great Britain at least every other year;
from that of August 12th we learn that he called upon Gilmer in Glasgow, but found him gone on an excursion.   In
this note the situation of professor of natural philosophy was
politely declined.   Buchanan (1790?–1852), we cannot doubt,
had been recommended by Leslie, whose favorite pupil he
was.   He had already, at the time Gilmer's offer was made,
won a considerable local reputation as a civil engineer, and
had also delivered lectures (1822) in Edinburgh on mechanical
philosophy.   His scientific reports on various government

enterprises and his success as an engineer, gave him sub-sequently a wide reputation—which was increased, among special students, by several well executed scientific treatises.

I must now go backwards, to give a letter written to Peachy Gilmer on the 31st of July, which, though mainly personal, seems worthy of presentation :

EDINBURGH, 31*st July*, 1824.

My dear Brother,

I have now been five days in the Metropolis of Scotland, one of the most beautiful cities of Europe, both in its natural scenery and admirable buildings, ... As I entered the town, and often since, I have had strange and melancholy reveries ; here fifty years ago, our father was at College, sport-ing with more than the usual gaiety of youth, here thirty-four years ago, our poor brother Walker caught his death like my ever beloved Harmer, by an assiduity, which there was no kind friend to temper—both their lives might have been saved, had those about them in their studies, possessed a spark of feeling or judgment—two lines in the poem which took the prize at Cambridge (which I heard recited) were equally applicable to H.

> " In learning's pure embrace he sank to rest
> Like a tired child, upon its mother's breast." [1]

But these reflections draw tears to my eyes for the millionth time, and each I resolve shall be the last, for they are vain.—

---

[1] Winthrop Mackworth Praed (1802-1839) of Trinity gained the Chan-cellor's medal in 1823 by his "Australasia," and in 1824 by his "Athens." In the latter poem the lines quoted occur. They commemorate the death of John Tweddel, a brilliant young Cantab, who died at Athens in 1799. It is sad to think that an early death cut off both the poet and his first American admirer from brilliant careers both in literature and in politics; and it is interesting to reflect that this is the first quotation from Praed that found its way to America—the country which had the honor of putting forth the first collection of his poems.

they no more than "honor's voice" can "provoke the silent
dust," or than "flattery soothe the dull, cold ear of death"
—when a few more heart strings are cut, I shall seem to belong
rather to the next world than to this, and without the saint like
purity of either of our brothers I shall be glad to lay my head
beside theirs—I write all this in no bitterness of heart nor in
any desponding mood, the place, the occasion and addressing
you from Edinburgh all conspire to elicit fruitless sighs.

My visit has so far been very pleasant, I told you what a
delightful time I had at Cambridge. I have since spent two
days with the celebrated Dr. Parr, the greatest scholar, now
in existence. He is old, decrepid, and with the manners of a
pedagogue, but withal, exceedingly agreeable. He is a decided
and warm champion of our country, took great interest in my
mission, and has already been of service in furnishing me a
catalogue of books. He spoke right out and said several very
flattering things to me, which it is not worth while to repeat
even to you. He went with me to Guy's Cliff (one of the
most romantic establishments in G. B.) and to Kenilworth,
where we dined with a friend of his.

The people of Edinburgh are very hospitable and kind,
but less like ourselves, than the Cambridge lads. Here every
man seems engaged in letters or science. I breakfasted with
the famous professor Leslie, and he was surrounded by his
meteorological machines.

Mr. Jefferson imagined he would be hostile to us. I have
turned him to good account, by having heard something (it
was very little) of his discoveries. . . . . Jeffrey is out of
town, but I shall see him. Mr. Murray a distinguished advo-
cate, connected with the great Lord Mansfield, has shown me
many civilities and I this morning received a written invitation to visit Lord Forbes,[1] which I shall not have time to do.

---

[1] Lord Forbes (1765–1843)—the seventeenth of the title and Premier
Baron of Scotland—had been somewhat distinguished as a soldier in his early
life. See a notice of him in the Gentleman's Magazine for 1843 (Part I).

He dined with us at Murray's yesterday, and is genteel and well disposed towards our country. I go from this place to London, and shall endeavour as soon as I can to draw matters to a close & return. I shall be able to turn the acquaintances I have made here to good account to our country. Even to procure a good library and apparatus is a great matter, for we then have at least the materials for working which we now want. They seem astonished to find I have been in G. B. only 6 or 7 weeks, and speak English quite as well as they, to say the least. I believe many of them on both sides the Tweed would give a good deal for my accent and articulation, which, I assure you, are nothing improved by this raw climate, which makes every one hoarse; they are generally less easy and fluent in conversation than we. . . . . .

Gilmer did see Jeffrey—for we have a note from the latter making proposals for a trip to Inverary and telling Gilmer to meet him in Glasgow. Putting this fact with the statement made in Buchanan's note, we are warranted in believing that the pleasant excursion was made. Besides we have a statement in one of the numerous letters before us that Mrs. Jeffrey wrote to her father in New York that Gilmer was the most popular and attractive American that had ever been seen in Edinburgh. I mentioned many pages back that Jeffrey was one of Ogilvie's auditors in New York; he was there in pursuit of this very Mrs. Jeffrey—then a Miss Wilkes—related, as De Quincey somewhere shows, to the celebrated Wilkes.

Although Gilmer does not seem to have visited Lord Forbes that gentleman was kind enough to send him three letters of introduction to literary friends in Dublin—whither Gilmer proposed to go if he did not succeed in Great Britain. His lordship's hand is not the best and I shall not risk pronouncing who his distinguished friends were.

Among the many invitations received by Gilmer while in Edinburgh was one from a Mr. Horner whom I take to have

been Leonard Horner the brother and biographer of Francis
Horner—the political economist and joint founder of the
Edinburgh Review.   If one only knew a few more facts
quite a pretty picture might be drawn of a pleasant, evening
spent by this clever young stranger in the presence of one
of the beauties of Great Britain.   But I do not know whether
Gilmer accepted the invitation or whether *Leonard* Horner
gave it or whether Mr. Horner was then married.   All that I
do know is that whenever he got Miss Lloyd[1] to marry him,
he got a beautiful woman.

   I now give the next letter written to Mr. Jefferson, in
which the professorship of law is finally declined.

EDINBURGH, Aug. 13th, 1884.

Dear Sir.

   It is now more than a fortnight since I arrived at the
Ancient Capitol of Scotland.   The first four or five days were
spent in making inquiries for persons fit for any of our purposes, but especially for anatomy, natural history, and natural
Philosophy ; for I had well satisfied myself in England that
we could not except by chance, procure either of the latter there.
In all Scotland, from all the men of letters or science at
Edinburgh, I could hear of but two, fit for any department, at
all likely to accept our proposals.   These were Mr. Buchanan
for natural philosophy, & Dr. Craigie[2] for anatomy &c.   I

---

[1] See Mrs. Gordon's "Christopher North," page 25.   Leonard Horner
(1785–1864) was a F. R. S. and a geologist of some note.   He was prominent in promoting the scheme for a university in London, and in 1827 was
made Warden of the new institution.

[2] David Craigie, M. D. (1793–1866) was a graduate of the University of
Edinburgh and (1832) fellow of the Edinburgh College of Physicians.   He
had not a large practice, nor was he famous as a teacher, but his "Elements
of General and Pathological Anatomy" (1828) is said to have shown great
reading and to be still valuable.   He was owner and editor of the Edinburgh Medical and Surgical Journal.   His health was continuously failing
for many years.

made to them both, and every where that I went, the most favourable representations I could with truth, of our University. They required time to consider of our offer.—and to day I have received the answers of both. They decline to accept it. You would be less astonished at this, if you knew what a change had taken place since you were in Europe. The professorships have become lucrative, beyond every thing. Even the Greek professor at Glasgow, Leslie tells me, receives 1500 guineas a year. Some of the lecturers here, receive above £4000 sterling. Besides this we have united branches which seem never to be combined in the same person in Europe. . . . . . I have moreover well satisfied myself, that taking all the departments of natural history, we shall at Philadelphia, New York &c procure persons more fit for our purpose than any where in G. B. The same may be said of Anatomy &c. I shall however set out for London to morrow, and try what can be done there by corresponding with the places I have visited. A mathematician and professor of ancient Languages we should, if possible, find in Europe, for they I am sure will be better than our own. Even here the difficulty is greater than you can conceive. Proficiency in Latin & Greek are still the sure passports to preferment both in Church & State; nor is the supply of men of the first eminence, or such as we must have, at all in proportion to the demand. When I came I thought it the easiest place to fill; I assure you it is far the most difficult. This Dr. Parr told me, but I thought he exaggerated the obstacles. I now believe he has not. You apprehended Leslie would be at best indifferent to us. He has however taken more interest in our success, than any one I have seen and been of more service to me. [Here he mentions Leslie's offer.]

.   .   .   .

I think it well to mention this, for the visitors may make something of it, and I believe if you were once to get him there, it would not be difficult to keep him.

It is time I should say something of the honor the visitors

have done me, though I have no more materials for deciding now, than when I left you. I make my decision, only to prevent delay in your looking elsewhere. I find it so doubtful, whether we can procure such persons as I should choose to be associated with; and thinking myself bound to make my election as early as possible, that I must say as the case now stands, I cannot accept the honor which has been conferred upon me, in a manner the most flattering, accompanied by a great mark of confidence in appointing me this most important mission. I shall discharge my undertaking to you and my duty to my country, perilous as it is, to satisfy my own conscience. I will, if it be possible in Europe, procure fit men; but I will rather return home, mortifying as it would be, without a single professor, than with mere impostors. As at present advised, I cannot say positively, that I may not be condemned to the humiliation of going back with Dr. Blaetterman only. All this is very discouraging to you, but I present to you the exact case, without any diplomacy to recommend myself or deceive you and my employers. Should they find fault with the address of their agent, they shall at least never condemn his honesty, or doubt his fidelity. My address (such as I possess) I shall reserve for my negotiations here.

This condition of affairs, requires all and much more than my fortitude—it mars all the pleasures of visiting Great Britain, tho' in my letters generally I preserve the appearance of good spirits and success, because I always look to the Legislature—I shall be happy if we can succeed and miserable to return without fulfilling all that you desired.

P. S. I assure you, Leslie will receive any communication from you as an honor, he is by no means hostile to Virginia. He speaks often of Col. R[andolph] with the utmost interest.

Having thus spent three pleasant weeks in Edinburgh, where he received attention from the distinguished men already named, as well as from Professor Jameson, the great geologist, Gilmer seems to have gone straight to London, where we find him on the 21st of August beginning a correspondence destined to be of great service to the University. Mr. Key, with whom Gilmer seems to have been staying, had recommended as classical professor a young college mate of his own—Mr. George Long. This gentleman was a year younger than Key, having been born in 1800. He was a fellow of Trinity, and already favorably known. I present a synopsis of Gilmer's letter to him as a specimen of the offer which the agent was authorized to make. He states that his powers are absolute, and that any engagement made with him would be binding without further ratification. Long is to have (1) a commodious house, garden, &c., entirely to himself, free of rent, (2) a salary of $1,500 and " tuition fees of from $50 to $25 from each pupil, according to the number of professors he attends." He can be removed only by the concurrent votes of five out of seven of the board of visitors. He is to be allowed to return to Cambridge in July, 1825, a concession necessary to his holding his fellowship. He is not to teach a grammar school, but advanced classes—Hebrew being included in his professorship, but with little chance of being required. The professors must be ready to sail by November. The letter concludes by explaining the site of the University, and is, as a whole, courteous and businesslike.[1] On the same day an almost exact counterpart of this letter was sent to the Rev. Henry Drury, assistant master of Harrow, who had been recommended by Dr. Parr, himself long connected with Harrow, as a fit person to advise in the matter of the classical professorship.

On the 24th of August, Gilmer wrote to Leslie an important letter of which I give the substance. Professor Jameson had advised that the object of the mission should be published in the leading newspapers. Gilmer thought that might do in

---

[1] It is given in Dr. Adams' monograph on Thomas Jefferson, page 114.

7

Scotland, but, remembering Brougham's admonitions, did not feel certain that it would work well in England, and so he felt compelled to decline Professor Jameson's offer to write up the matter. Jameson had also recommended Dr. Knox of Edinburgh for the anatomical chair; and as Gilmer did not know the latter's address, he requests Jameson to sound him on the subject. Leslie seems to have seconded Brougham's recommendation of Ivory, but Gilmer has not been able to find him and thinks he will secure Key's services instead. The letter closes by making a suggestion to Leslie about a physical experiment the latter had shown him in Edinburgh.

On the same day this letter was written, Mr. Long in Liverpool was writing a reply to Gilmer's offer of the 21st instant. His manly letter is given at length :—

LIVERPOOL, *August* 24.

The subject of your letter renders an apology for writing to me quite unnecessary; I am pleased with the plain & open manner in which you express yourself and encouraged by this I shall freely state to you all my thoughts on the subject, and make such enquiries as the case seems to me to admit. The nature of the powers with which you are vested gives me full confidence in your proposals, and from Mr. Key's letter I am led to expect that all information you give me will bear the same marks as the communication I have already received. The peculiar circumstances of my situation induce me to throw off all reserve, and to trouble you with more words than otherwise would be necessary. About two years since I lost my remaining parent, a mother whose care and attention amply compensated for the loss of a father & no inconsiderable property in the West India Islands. By this unfortunate occurrence I have the guardianship of a younger brother, and two younger sisters thrown upon me—with numerous difficulties, which it is useless to mention because no body but myself can properly judge of them,—and with an income for their support which is rapidly diminishing in value. I have for some time past been directing my attention to the study of the law with the hopes of improving my fortune, and the ambition, which I hope is a laudable one, of rising in my profession. In truth the latter is almost my only motive for entering into the profession, as I am well acquainted with the insupportable tedium & vexation of the practical part. But the obstacles in my way, tho I should consider them trifling if I were solely concerned for myself, become formidable when I reflect on the situation of my family. I wish then to know if that part of America would afford an asylum for a family that has been accustomed to live in a respectable manner, and an opportunity for laying out a little property to advantage.

From your account of that part of Virginia, and from what I have learned from books and other sources of information, I conclude that new comers are not liable to be carried off by any dangerous epidemic disorder.

The salary attached to the professorship seems adequate . . . . but I wish to know what proportion it bears to the expense of living—many of the common articles of food I can imagine to be as cheap as in England—but other articles such as wearing apparel, furniture & I should conceive to be dearer than they are here. Your information on this subject will supply the defects in mine.

Is the University placed on such a footing as to ensure a permanent and durable existence, or is the scheme so far an experiment that there is a possibility of its failing?

Is there any probability of the first Professor being enabled to double the 1500 dollars, when the University is fairly set at work, by his tuition fees? You will perhaps be surprised at this question; I am not at all mercenary or addicted to the love of money—I have reasons for asking which I could better explain in a personal interview.

Is there in the county of Albemarle, or town of Charlottes-ville, tolerably agreeable society, such as would in some degree compensate for almost the only comfort an Englishman would hesitate [to] leave behind him?

What vacations would the Professor have—and at what seasons of the year—of what nature, with respect to the time to be left for literary pursuits, and the studies connected with his profession, by which as much might be effected as by the employment more immediately attached to the situation?

With respect to my coming to England in 1825, that would be absolutely necessary. Unless I take the degree of Master of Arts next July, I forfeit my Fellowship which is at present the only means of subsistence I have, except the occupation in which I am at present engaged of taking private pupils. Should the expectation that I am induced to form be realized, my Fellowship of course would be a small consideration: but as I just observed the settlement of my affairs here would render my presence necessary in 1825.

The Professors, you tell me, can only be removed by the concurring voice of 5 out of the 7 directors: I presume that inability to perform the duties of the office, or misconduct would be the only points on which such a removal would be attempted.

I have no attachment to England as a country: it is a delightful place for a man of rank and property to live in, but I was not born in that enviable station . . . If comfortably settled therefore in America I should never wish to leave it.

I wish to know what may be the expenses of the voyage & if they are to be defrayed by the persons engaged—also what kind of an outfit would be necessary, I mean merely for a person's own convenience.

Mr. Key knows nothing of me but from college acquaintance: he therefore could not know that he was directing you to a person who would raise so many difficulties, and make so many enquiries some of which you may judge impertinent. For the last 6 years I have struggled with pecuniary difficulties, & I am not yet quite free from them: I have thus learned at an early age to calculate expenses, & consider probabilities: when I know the whole of a case, I can come to a determination & abide by it.

If you will favor me with an answer as soon as you find it convenient, I shall consider it a great favor—I must again apologize for the freedom with which I have expressed myself: when I have received your letter, I will inform you of my determination.

I will thank you to inform Mr. Key that he will receive a letter from me by the next post after that which brings yours.

I remain with the greatest respect

Yours   G. Long.

Please to direct "George Long, No. 1 King St., Soho, Liverpool.

In the meantime Gilmer, on the advice of Dr. Parr, had written on the subject of the classical professorship to Samuel Butler (1774–1839), the well-known head master of Shrewsbury school. Dr. Butler was one of the leading English educators, and a great friend of Dr. Parr's, whose funeral sermon he preached. After a brilliant career at Cambridge, where he was elected Craven scholar over Coleridge, he had taken charge of the Shrewsbury school in 1798, and made it one of the best in the country. He was a noted classical scholar, and was at this very time finishing his edition of Aeschylus. He was subsequently made Bishop of Lichfield and Coventry.

Dr. Butler answered Gilmer on the 26th of August, and recommended in high terms a clergyman whose name he did not give. He also assured Gilmer that he would be glad to show him the school[1] and give him further information, adding that although he could not offer him a bed, he should be happy to see him at breakfast, dinner, and supper.

---

[1] A glance through the Rev. J. Pycroft's "Oxford Memories" will show how high the Shrewsbury boys stood in the classics. In athletics they were backward; for it was to them that Eton sent the famous message when challenged for a cricket (or football) match: "Harrow we know, and Winchester we know, but who are ye?"

On the next day (the 27th) Gilmer wrote two letters, one to
Mr. Long, the other to Mr. Jefferson. That to Long
answered his queries *seriatim,* and, as its writer observed, dealt
with him not as a merchant, but rather as a scholar. He was
to teach Latin, Greek, Hebrew, Rhetoric, and Belles-Lettres ;
but little stress was to be laid on the three last.

The letter to Jefferson runs as follows :

LONDON, 27th Aug., 1824.

Dear Sir,

My last letter from Edinburgh gave so gloomy an account
of our prospects, that I hasten to relieve the picture. When
I saw needy young men living miserably up 10 or 12 stories
in the wretched climate of Edinburgh, reluctant to join us, I
did not know where we could expect to raise recruits. While
at Cambridge I became acquainted in Trinity College with an
intelligent and fine young man, distinguished even at Cambridge for his mathamatical genius and attainments, and M.
A. of that University. He is the son of an eminent physician of London, and I hardly hoped we should induce him
to go with us. I have, however, done so, and am delighted
to find him a great enthusiast for the United States, and
exactly fitted to our purposes in every respect. Securing him
is a great matter, for he has a high character with the young
men who were with him at Cambridge, and he will assist in
procuring others. Already he has suggested the most fit
person for the classics, and I am enquiring of others about
him. The departments of anatomy, natural history and natural philosophy will then only remain. I have had more
persons recommended for anatomy than for any other place,
but immediately they find they will not be allowed to practice
medicine, &c., abroad, they decline proceeding further. That
I fear will prove an insurmountable obstacle to us in this
department. In the other two, I shall have great difficulties, and far from being harassed by applications, I
cannot hear of any one at all likely to answer our purpose.

With a good classic, an able master of experimental science, and Key for our mathematician, we shall be strong whatever the rest may be.

The books and apparatus now occupy me very much—at the same time, I am corresponding with all parts of the kingdom, about professors. On returning to London, I received two letters from my venerable friend Dr. Parr, and another from his grand-son (who will be his executor) proposing to sell us the Doctor's Library entire at his death. It is a rich and rare and most valuable collection of the classics. But I wrote to them that the amount would be greater than I could apply to this single department. I promised however to suggest it to the Visitors, and if they please they can enter into correspondence on the subject. . . . . . It would give some eclat perhaps to our Institution to have the Doctor's Library. I am not without hope of opening the campaign in February with some splendors. I know the importance of complete success with the next legislature and shall consider that in every thing I do.

I have been seeking Ivory all over London, but such is the state of science among alderman and "freemen," that no one can tell me where he is or ever even heard of him, and in Edinburgh, I found a splendid monument to Lord Melville and none to Napier or Burns. In Westminster Abbey, there is none to Bacon or Blake, but a great many to state and ecclesiastical impostors.

I shall write more at length as soon as I have done more. I wrote this only to allay your apprehensions excited by my last.

I have seen Major Cartwright, who is old and infirm. Dugald Stewart has lost the musick of his eloquent tongue by paralysis; he lives near Linlithgow about 20 miles from Edinburgh, is averse to company, and I therefore enclosed your letter with a card, expressing my regret that the state of his health should deprive me of the honor of his acquaintance.

Dr. Parr was delighted with your letter and will no
doubt give me one for you, &c.

The visit to Major Cartwright brought Gilmer an invitation to dinner which bears the date of August 30th. Some
description of this remarkable character might not be out of
place, as the name of his brother, the inventor, is much more
familiar to the majority of readers than his own. But space
is wanting, and after all he intended far more good than he
accomplished. Nevertheless as naval officer, losing the chance
of promotion by his sympathy with America, as an agitator
for the reform of parliament, as a colleague of Clarkson's, as
a distinguished agriculturist, and as a sympathizer with the
Spanish patriots, he deserves to be remembered, and was, as
Mr. Jefferson said, a most worthy character for Gilmer
to meet. Although the veteran (1740–1824) was within
a month of his death, he busied himself greatly in behalf of
Gilmer's mission. He got Mr. Harris, the former secretary to
the Royal Institution, to make out a list of such editions as
should be chosen for the University library, and he wrote to
Bentham for a catalogue of the latter's works and bespoke his
interest in Gilmer. Whether the philosopher knew that the
young American had four years ago *confuted* him, is a matter
of uncertainty—certain it is, however, that the desired catalogue was forthcoming. The Major also sent Gilmer a copy
of his "English Constitution Produced and Illustrated,"
which, if it be as dry, as it is represented to be, I hope
the young man did not feel bound to read.

In the meantime Gilmer had been introduced to a person
destined to be of the greatest assistance to him. This was
no other than Dr. George Birkbeck (1776–1841), the celebrated founder of the Glasgow Mechanics' Institute, said
to have been the first of its kind in the world. Dr. Birkbeck's interest in popular education began in 1800, when
he delivered a course of lectures to workingmen in Glasgow. He had left Glasgow for London in 1804, and had

practised medicine for many years; but he had taken up the
cause of education again, and was in this very year (1824)
elected the first president of the London Mechanics' Institute,
afterwards called in his honor the Birkbeck Institute. He
was one of the founders of the University of London,—a
fact which we shall have occasion to remember.

Dr. Birkbeck's first letter to Gilmer was dated the 29th of
August, and addressed to him at 3, Warwick St., Charing
Cross. In it attention was drawn to a gentleman destined to
form the third member of the new faculty—Dr. Robley Dunglison, a prominent physician of Scotch extraction, residing
in London. Dr. Dunglison, then about 26 years of age, was
already favorably known as a medical writer, a reputation
which, it is almost needless to say, was widely extended
after he settled in this country. Gilmer was not long in following up Dr. Birkbeck's suggestion; for on September 5th
Dr. Dunglison finally accepted the anatomical professorship.

The first of September brought a note from Major Cartwright, together with four of his political tracts which, the
writer declared, were with no small satisfaction put into the
hands of a gentleman then occupied in collecting materials for
perpetuating and adorning Republican Freedom. From the
same note we see that Gilmer was to dine with him on the
morrow. I may remark that Mr. Jefferson's letter to Cartwright was delivered by Gilmer, and is to be found in the
second volume of Francis Dorothy Cartwright's life of her
uncle (London, 1826, page 265). This letter is very interesting, and contains a complimentary notice of Gilmer.

On the 2nd of September the assistant master of Harrow
(Rev. Henry Drury) answered Gilmer's letter of August 21st
in a very formal note. He stated that he had been in the
south of France, hence his delay, and that he had no one as
yet to propose. He promised, however, to write to Dr. Parr,
and hoped to answer more satisfactorily in a few days. He
also mentioned that a similar application had been made to
him some years ago concerning Boston—by Mr. Rufus King,

whose sons were his pupils.   At that time he had had no one
in view.

On the same day Mr. Long wrote. from Liverpool, gratefully accepting Gilmer's offer.   He had conversed with Adam
Hodgson, a Liverpool merchant, who had written some letters on America, and his report of Charlottesville had settled
the matter.   Like all of Long's letters, this one was straight-
forward and manly.

Leslie also wrote on the 2nd of September regretting that
no public announcement of the mission had been made and
throwing a slight damper upon the whole scheme.   He promised to speak to Dr. Knox[1] and seemed to favor him.   Gilmer's
suggestion as to the experiment was received with some little
contempt, but the philosopher promised to do his best in help-
ing him to get good instruments.   He cited the case of the
University of Christiania which, in so poor a country as Nor-
way, "had £1000 at first furnished for instruments and £200
per annum since."

It has already been mentioned that on September 5th Dr.
Dunglison definitely accepted.   He desired to add chemistry
to his chair of anatomy, but this request was afterwards
refused.   On the 6th Gilmer answered Long's letter of accept-

---

[1] Dr. Robert Knox, then about 35 years old, was one of the best known
of the Edinburgh physicians and owned one of the finest private anatomical collections in Europe.   He did not come to America; but it would have
been better for him if he had.   Readers of the *Noctes Ambrosianæ* will
surely remember the account of the famous Burke and Hare murder trial
given in the number for March, 1829.   Burke and Hare had committed
several shocking murders in 1828, for the sole purpose of furnishing this
Dr. Knox with subjects.   It was claimed that the bodies were brought to
Knox in such a fresh condition that he must have had suspicions of foul
play.   Burke was hanged, Hare having turned state's evidence.   The
excitement was immense, Knox's house was sacked by the mob and at
Burke's execution thousands were heard crying: "Where are Knox and
Hare?"   Knox betook himself to London where he became an itinerant
lecturer on ethnology.   See Dr. McKenzie's edition of the *Noctes*, III, 239,
&c. (New York, 1875).

ance and assured him that the University would not be sectarian —a thing which Long had feared. On the day before (the 5th) which was Sunday, Gilmer had been to Woolwich to see Peter Barlow, the celebrated professor at the Royal Military Academy; but not finding him returned at once to London.

On the 7th Barlow wrote regretting that he had missed his visit and answering a letter which Gilmer had left. This letter concerned one of the professorships which had been very difficult to fill—that of natural philosophy. Mr. Barlow was certainly the person to apply to. Born in 1776 of obscure parents, he had worked his way through many difficulties and was now among the foremost scientists of his day. His valuable tables, his essay on the strength of materials, and his magnetical discoveries had gained him great applause and considerable emoluments. He had just (1823) been elected a fellow of the Royal Society and was about to get the Copley medal (1825) for his magnetic discoveries. From 1827 he was destined to do valuable work as an optician and the Barlow lens has perpetuated his name. He died in 1862 having long since resigned his professorship. In the present letter Barlow proposed to write to a gentleman, whose name he withheld, and sound him on the subject of the required professorship. His nominee was stated to be the son of a late distinguished mathematical professor known both in England and America. This seems to point to Charles Bonnycastle, son of John Bonnycastle, the great mathematical professor at Woolwich, whose books were certainly used at that time in America, and who had been dead about three years. But Barlow's note of September 22nd shows that he had been corresponding with Mr. George Harvey, of Plymouth, about the same place. The only explanation is that Professor Barlow found that Mr. Bonnycastle was abroad on some business for the government, and as Gilmer was in a hurry, suggested Mr. Harvey as the next best choice. It will be seen that subsequently Mr. Bonnycastle obtained the place.

On the 9th, Dr. Butler wrote from Shrewsbury asking

many questions in behalf of his clerical friend. Some of these questions show considerable acquaintance with matters purely secular, but I have not time to dilate upon them. The letter, of course, did no good, as Long had already accepted.

Mr. Drury, of Harrow, also wrote on the same day about the same professorship—this time he did recommend somebody, viz., his brother[1]—in highly eulogistic terms. To the credit of the gentleman it must, however, be said that he did not attempt to conceal the fact that his brother was in pecuniary embarrassments and hence anxious to get away. This letter, too, must be added to the futile correspondence of which the volumes before me are full.

In the meantime Dr. Birkbeck had recommended for the chair of natural history, the hardest of all to fill, Dr. John Harwood, who was a lecturer before the Royal Institution and who was then giving a course of lectures before a scientific society in Manchester. This recommendation led to a long correspondence, the discussion of which I shall put off for a time, as it was mixed enough to involve Gilmer in some perplexity and his biographer in more.

On September 11th Mr. Barlow wrote that he was quite at a loss to know why he had not heard from his friend Mr. Bonnycastle (?). He proposed to wait on Gilmer in London, on the following Monday (13th), unless that gentleman could take a family dinner with him on the next day—Sunday—when they would have an opportunity of discussing matters

---

[1] The Rev. Benjamin Heath Drury (namesake of a former distinguished head master), then at Eton, subsequently Vicar of Tugby, Lincolnshire. He died Feb. 20, 1835, and was a son of the Rev. Joseph Drury, long head master of Harrow and the friend of Lord Byron.

The Rev. Henry Joseph Thomas Drury (M.A., F.R.S., F.S.A.) had been a fellow of King's, Cambridge, was greatly interested in the Roxburghe Club, and possessed one of the finest libraries of the Greek classics in England. This library he was compelled to sell by auction at different times. He died March 5th, 1841, in his 63rd year. See *Gentleman's Magazine* for that year, also the chapter on Harrow in T. A. Trollope's "What I Remember."

more freely than by letter. Whether this invitation was accepted does not appear; but it would seem that some communication was had which led to the Harvey correspondence.

Between the eleventh and the eighteenth of September we find only one letter received by Gilmer. This was a pleasant one from Dugald Stewart, written from his retreat at Kinneil House, Linlithgowshire. It is such a perfect specimen of its kind that I must make room for it. Stewart, the reader will remember, had been paralyzed in 1822. His retreat in Linlithgowshire had been due to the generosity of a friend, and he was enjoying an ample pension, which John Wilson, who in 1820 had taken Dr. Brown's place in the Edinburgh University, and hence was Stewart's co-joint professor, was mean enough to criticize. The death of his son in 1809 had greatly prostrated him, and left him with an only daughter, in whose handwriting the following letter is:

KINNEIL HOUSE BY BO-NESS, N. B., *Sept.* 14*th*, 1824.

Sir,

It was with much regret I learnt from your note, that you had left Scotland without giving me an opportunity of meeting with you; and altho' I feel very grateful for the kind motive which deprived me of that pleasure, I cannot help expressing to yourself how very seriously I felt the disappointment. My indisposition would indeed have made my share of the conversation next to nothing, but I would have listened with great eagerness and interest to your information about America and in particular about Mr. Jefferson, who I am happy to find from his letter has not forgotten me after so long and so eventful an interval. I need not add that I should have enjoyed a real satisfaction in being personally known to a Gentleman of whom Mr. Jefferson speaks in such flattering terms, and to whose sole discernment has been committed the important trust of selecting the Professors for the new University.

I was truly sorry to learn that you had not succeeded in finding any recruits at Edinburgh for your new College. The field I should have thought, a very ample one, more especially in the medical department. I hope you have been more fortunate in the English Universities and should be extremely happy to hear from you on the subject. It is impossible for Mr. Jefferson himself to take a more anxious concern than I do, in everything connected with the prosperity of the United States, and particularly in every scheme which aims at improving the System of Education in that part of the world. May I beg to be informed about your own plans and when you propose to recross the Atlantic. Is there no chance of your taking your departure from a Scotch Port? If you should, I might still indulge the hope of seeing you here. At all events I shall write to Mr. Jefferson. I am sorry to think that my good wishes are all I have to offer for his infant establishment.

With much regard I am, dear sir,

Your most obedient servant,

DUGALD STEWART.

FRANCES WALKER GILMER, Esq.

The interval before mentioned was probably employed by Gilmer in visiting distinguished men, among whom was Campbell, whom he greatly admired, and certainly in writing the following letters—the first to Mr. Jefferson, the second to Dabney Carr:

LONDON, 15th Sept., 1824.

My Dear Sir

I have given you so much bad news, that I determined to delay writing a few days that I might communicate something more agreeable.

When I returned from Edinburgh, where my ill success is in part to be ascribed (I am well assured) to the ill will of some of our eastern Brethren, who had just before me been

in Scotland, I determined to remain at London as the most
convenient point for correspondence.   Here assisted by Key
our mathematician (with whom I am more pleased the more
I see of him) and several men of character and learning, I
have been busily engaged since I last wrote.   I have had the
good fortune to enlist with us for the ancient languages a
learned and highly respectable Cantab., but there have been
two obstacles that have made me pause long before I conclude
with him.   He has no knowledge of Hebrew, which is to be
taught at the University.   This I easily reconciled to my duty,
from the absolute necessity of the case.   Oriental literature is
very little esteemed in England, and we might seek a whole
year and perhaps, not at last find a real Scholar in Latin and
Greek who understands Hebrew.   The other difficulty is more
serious.   Mr. Long, the person I mean, is an alumnus of
Trinity College, Cambridge, he is entitled to his fellowship
only on condition of his presenting himself at the meeting in
the first week in July next.   Failure to do this, no matter
under what circumstances, will deprive him of about £300
per annum.   That would be a great sacrifice.   Still he seemed
to me so decidedly superior to his competitors, who do not lie
under the incapacity of being of clerical character, that I believe
I shall not be faithful to my trust if I do not engage him
with a reservation of the privilege of being at Cambridge for
a week *only* in July; that is my present impression and very
strongly fixed, tho' there was another most competent professor
I could have, but for his being a clergyman.   The Professor
of Anatomy &c is a very intelligent and laborious gentleman,
a Dr. Dunglison, now of London, and a writer of considerable
eminence on various medical and anatomical subjects.

The Professors of natural philosophy and of natural history,
still remain to be procured. . . . . .   Another week will inform me what can be done about the two vacant chairs.

The library and apparatus have given me great difficulty
and trouble.   I delayed as long as possible speaking for them,
to have the assistance of the professors.·   But the time for

shipping them now presses so close, I have made out a catalogue of such as we must have, and have ordered the books and instruments to be shipped as soon as possible. The present aspect of affairs assures me, we shall be able to open the University on the 1st of February as you desired. The professors vary in age from about 26 to 43 or 4. Blaettermann is already married and by a very singular coincidence wholly unknown to me at the time, each of the others tho' now unmarried, will take out a young English wife,[1] tho' if they would take my advice they would prefer Virginians notwithstanding.

Dr. Parr has engaged to marry me in England without his fee which here is often considerable.

Having already declined the honor so flatteringly conferred upon me, I no longer feel at liberty to express any wish upon the subject. But really every thing promises to make a Professorship at the University one of the most pleasant things imaginable.

I have had no assistance (I wish I could say that were all) from a single American, now in England. Leslie in Scotland and Dr. Birkbeck (cousin to the Illinois Birkbeck) of London have taken most interest in the matter.

Mackintosh is too lazy for anything and Brougham's letters introduced me to eminent men, but they never took the right way, or to the right means for us, they talk of plate, furniture &c for the pavilions, while we want men for work.

I have had but a single letter from America—that gave me the very agreeable news, that you were all well in Albermarle, &c.

LONDON, 19*th Sept.*, 1824.

My dear friend,

Many accidents have conspired to delay my embarcation for Virginia longer than I wished; at this season of the year no man in England is where he ought to be, except perhaps

---

[1] It does not appear that either Long or Bonnycastle carried out wives.

those of the Fleet & of Newgate. Every little country school
master, who never saw a town, is gone, as they say, to the
country, that is to Scotland to shoot grouse, to Doncaster to
see a race, or to Cheltenham to dose himself with that vile
water. With all these difficulties and not only without assistance but with numerous enemies to one's success (as every
Yankee in England is) I have done wonders. I have employed four Professors of the most respectable families, of real
talent, learning &c &c a fellow of Trinity Col. Camb. and
a M. A. of the same University. Then they are Gentlemen,
and what should not be overlooked they all go to Virginia
with the most favourable prepossessions towards our Country.
If learning does not raise its drooping head it shall not be my
fault. For myself I shall return to the bar with recruited
health and redoubled vigour. I shall study and work &
speak & do something at last that shall redound to the honor
of my country. My intercourse with professional and Literary men here has fired again all my boyish enthusiasm, and I
pant to be back and at work. The library of the University
and my intimacy with the professors, will now make even my
summer holidays a period of study. Virginia must still be
the great nation; she has genious enough, she wants only
method in her application. I have seen several of the most
eminent Scotch & English lawyers, and you may rely upon
it, our first men have nothing to fear from a comparison with
the best of them. The only decided advantage any of them
have over us, is in Brougham. He has more science & accu-
rate information (not letters mark you) than any one who
ever figured at the English bar or in Parliament. In the
mathematics, physical sciences, and political economy, few
even of their exclusive professors are so learned; his labor is
endless, his memory retentive, his faculties quick. I have
not seen him at full stretch, but I think his mind is more
like that of Calhoun, than any of our men. Mackintosh
passes for very little here; he is lazy to excess, always vacil-
lating and undecided, is allowed to have a great memory,

8

much curious learning &c but is without the promptness and
tact necessary to business; then no one can rely on his opinions, principles or exertions.   He is either not present or
takes exactly the opposite course from what every one sup-
poses he will.   His declamatory way of talking about the
"extraordinary eccentricities of the human mind" &c seems
after such endless repetitions, monotonous & cold, while his
manner is nearly as bad as any manner can be—swaggering
vociferations and ear-splitting violence from beginning to end.[1]

The University will open in February and I shall be with
you in time to give you a greeting at the Court of Appeals.

.   .   .   .

Another way in which Gilmer employed his time was in
examining the library at Lambeth.   Having wished to have
a MS. relating to the life of John Smith copied, he entered
into correspondence with one of the librarians and was successful in his object.   This copy ought to be in the library of
the University of Virginia, but I can learn nothing of it.[2]

On the 19th a sad little note was received from Miss Frances
Dorothy Cartwright whom Gilmer had met at her uncle's
house.   Major Cartwright, who had now only four days to
live, had directed that a package of his writings should be
made up, and carried to Mr. Jefferson by Gilmer.   In sending this his niece took occasion to write a loving and pathetic
note about her uncle's condition and to express herself as glad
that Gilmer would be able to speak of him as he deserved,
in a country he had always loved.   The note is touching and
bespoke the true feminine heart which had burst forth into
song over the woes of the Spaniards.   For the lady was not
only a devoted niece and faithful biographer but a poetess,

---

[1] Compare with his friend Ticknor's impression (Ticknor's Life, &c.,
1, 289).

[2] At the end of George Long's biographical sketch of Marcus Aurelius
there is an eloquent tribute to Smith.   It is highly probable that Gilmer
introduced the great Captain to Long's notice.

albeit her works have not given her fame. She was the daughter of the distinguished inventor and lived to a ripe old age—dying in 1863.

On the 20th of September Mr. George Harvey wrote from Plymouth, asking many questions about the University. On the 22nd Peter Barlow wrote a short and unimportant note about Mr. Harvey, and on the 25th that gentleman himself wrote from Plymouth declining, on family considerations, gratefully, but positively, the chair of natural philosophy.[1] In the meantime the correspondence with Harwood about the professorship of natural history had been going on vigorously.

On the 27th Mr. Rush wrote proposing a visit to the dockyard at Portsmouth during the first week in October ; and as Gilmer wrote to his brother Peachy from that port on October 4th, the visit was probably made.

Dr. Parr also wrote, on the same day, a characteristic letter, which is here inserted :

HATTON, *3rd Oct.,* 1824.

Dear & much respected Mr. Gillmar,

I have been very ill, but I hope to be better. I will give myself the sweet satisfaction of writing to you a few lines before you leave England. I rejoice to hear that you have fixed upon proper teachers and I beg at your leisure that you will inform me of your names, the schools where they have been educated & the persons who have recommended them. When I get more strength & have the aid of a scribe I shall

---

[1] Among the obituary notices in the Gentleman's Magazine I came across one which seems to point to this gentleman. It was to the effect that on October 29th, 1834, George Harvey, Esq., one of the mathematical masters at Woolwich, committed suicide in Plymouth by hanging himself by a silk handkerchief from a hook in his cellar—"verdict, mental derangement." Mr. Harvey contributed studies to various philosophical magazines, and two of his contributions may be found in the 10th volume of the Proceedings of the Royal Society of Edinburgh.

write to you and to Mr. Jefferson, and I shall correspond with
both of you unreservedly.   Through an active life and [of]
nearly seventy eight [years] I have experienced the precious
advantages of steadiness & sincerity.   This you would have
seen clearly if you had known me more closely.   Mr. Gilmar,
there is now a safe & open path for mutual communication
thro' the American Ambassador & you will prepare occasionally for forwarding our letters.   To Mr. Jefferson present not
only my good wishes but the tribute of my respect & my confidence.   I shall write of him [what] Dr. Young said of
Johnson's Rasselas—"It was a globe of sense."   I use the
same words with the same approbation of Mr. Jefferson's letter to me.   I have corresponded with many scholars, many
philosophers, & many eminent politicians upon many subjects,
but never, and I repeat the word, never did I see a more
wise letter than that with which I was honored by Mr.
Jefferson.   I shall preserve it as [here the letter is torn]
I heartily wish you a good voyage and have the honour to
subscribe myself,

Dear Sir, your faithful friend &

Respectful obedient servant,

SAMUEL PARR.

By a letter from Key received on September 27th, we learn
that the contracts with the four professors already engaged
were being signed.   There were, of course, some hitches with
all, but both sides were anxious to be fair, and the difficulties
were soon removed.   A copy of the covenant with Dr. Dunglison is before me, but I am not certain that it was not
altered, for it was made before any signatures had been
affixed.   The first year's salary was fixed at $1,500; for the
next four years it might vary from $1,000 to $1,500, accord-
ing to the amount realized by tuition fees; the other provisions need not be cited.   From Key's letter we find that both
Dr. Dunglison and himself had engaged passage from Liverpool on the 16th of October.

On the same day, September 27th, a short note from Dugald Stewart was received, with a letter for Mr. Jefferson, and wishes for Gilmer's pleasant voyage.

In the meantime Dr. John Harwood, although his own plans with regard to the University were undecided, had suggested Mr. Frederick Norton, of Bristol, as a proper person for the chair of natural philosophy ; and Gilmer had written to him accordingly. On October 3rd, Mr. Norton wrote to Gilmer asking for further information. I have been unable to get any information as to Mr. Norton's antecedents.

About this time Mr. Gilmer received the following letter, which requires some comment :

10 Seymour Street West.

My dear Sir

I thought I could let you go back to America without troubling you with a letter for my brother. I could not well dwell at length on the painful subject of my boy's state but I have alluded to it. In case it should give pain to his affectionate heart too much on my account, you may tell him that habit & fortitude are beginning to reconcile me even to this most terrible blow that ever befell my existence. You can tell him how cheerful you saw me & I am habitually so—for I think it folly to grieve at fate.

He is to be removed [to] an asylum very soon. At present he is in so strange a state that it is painful to see company in my own House. This circumstance has debarred me from the pleasure of shewing you many attentions that were due to you as a mark of my sense of your kindness. I have been much gratified however by making your acquaintance & with best wishes for your safety & happiness remain,

Dear Sir,
Yours very truly,
T. Campbell.

The son whose misfortune is alluded to was Thomas
Telford, named after Campbell's friend, the distinguished
engineer. The poet's grief was great, and besides his work
upon "Theodoric," which was published in November of
this year, he threw himself heart and soul into another
piece of work, to drive away his cares. This was the agi-
tation of a scheme for establishing a university in London.
Some such project had been in his mind since his visit to
Germany in 1820; but it was not brought prominently
forward until January 31st, 1825, at a dinner given by
Brougham.[1] The matter was then pressed warmly by
Brougham, Joseph Hume, Dr. Birkbeck, and others, and
was brought to a successful issue in 1827. Now, as Campbell had allowed the idea to rest for five years, I do not think
it at all improbable that Gilmer's visit, connected as it was
with a similar movement in a kindred country, had a great
deal to do with giving a fresh impetus to the scheme. Then,
too, Gilmer had been thrown into intimate relations with
Brougham and Dr. Birkbeck, and probably with Leonard
Horner, and had doubtless by his enthusiasm kindled afresh
their own natural impulses toward educational work—and
these three were prominent among the founders of the London
University. Besides there is a striking parallel in the un-
theological basis of both colleges. It is well known that this
latter institution drew back two of the professors whom England had lent to America; but it is more than probable that
the connection between the two universities began with Gilmer's visit.

But to return to our main theme. Only four professors
have so far been secured—those of natural philosophy and of
natural history remain. The latter professorship was not
filled at all in England, and the correspondence about it will
occupy us soon. The former was filled before Gilmer left

[1] See the article on Campbell in the Dictionary of National Biography,
and also Beattie's Life of Campbell.

England, by the selection of Mr. Charles Bonnycastle, who
has been mentioned before.   Mr. Bonnycastle was then in his
33rd year, and was engaged abroad on some government business, the nature of which I have not learned.   No letters to
or from him are preserved, although some were written ; the
whole matter seems to have been arranged between Gilmer
and Peter Barlow, after the 25th of September, when Mr.
Harvey definitely declined.   Gilmer, however, seems to have
had a conversation with Bonnycastle just before he left London.   This hasty arrangement by proxy led to a slight misunderstanding, as will be seen in the next chapter.   A short
account of the Harwood correspondence will close our sketch
of Mr. Gilmer's important mission.

On the 20th of September, Dr. John Harwood, then
lecturing in Manchester, answered a letter which Gilmer had
been advised to write by Dr. Birkbeck.   In this answer he
expatiates on the advantages such a new field as America
would offer a natural historian, but regrets that an engagement
to lecture before the Royal Institution will leave him undecided as to his plans until the following May.   But he
offers a suggestion that may obviate the difficulty.   He has a
brother now studying medicine in Edinburgh, who has been
a fellow lecturer with him in natural history, and who is
zealous in the cause.   Why not let him keep the place warm?
He can have copies of any lectures the Doctor himself would
deliver; and if the latter decide to remain in England,
no fitter person than the brother can be found to keep the
chair, and in two countries two Harwoods can work their
way to fame.   Gilmer's answer to this really well-worded
letter, has not been preserved ; but from a letter written by
Harwood on September 20th, I judge that it was not unfavor-
able.   The Doctor talks of forming a nucleus for a museum
at once, and promises to look out for a professor of natural
philosophy.   Then comes a long and manly letter from William Harwood, the brother, offering his services.   He owns to
no very extensive knowledge of mineralogy, but has a good

training in chemistry, and is especially fond of zöology. He asks sensible questions, and writes throughout in a modest tone.

In the meantime (September 26th) John Harwood wrote, mentioning Norton by residence but not by name, and giving valuable information with regard to the purchase of a museum. He also recommends his brother in warm terms. Gilmer wrote, complaining that Harwood was not explicit enough, although to my mind he very explicitly wished his brother to get the place, either permanently or temporarily. Then Dr. Harwood wrote a letter on September 30th, "respectfully observing" that *he* could not enter into *any foreign engagement* for the *present*, but that his brother was at liberty to made arrangements either permanent or temporary. On October 1st, Dr. Harwood wrote another letter, this time concerning Norton, who would like the place, and whom he recommended highly, observing, however, that he was by no means a man of the world.   Then on October 24th the Doctor wrote to his friend, Birkbeck, and stated that William Harwood had undertaken, at Gilmer's request, a visit to the Isle of Wight, to see that gentleman on his way out. On his arrival there, Gilmer informed him that so much time had elapsed that he should prefer to leave the matter to the Board of Visitors, unless Harwood would go out at his own risk. Dr. Harwood himself went over to Liverpool, in hopes of seeing Gilmer, but saw only Mr. Long. We learn also that Mr. Norton went to the Isle of Wight to see Gilmer, but arrived four hours too late—a sad commentary on unworldliness. This letter was forwarded by Dr. Birkbeck to Gilmer, in Virginia. Next in series comes a letter dated and endorsed *November* 16th, which can only mean *September* 16, but which is unimportant. It may here be remarked, incidentally, that in forwarding Harwood's letter, Dr. Birkbeck spoke highly of Bonnycastle, and stated that had he had any idea that the young man was within Gilmer's reach, he would have been his first recommendation.

Now it is not well to offer opinions when one has read only one side of the case, and I know Mr. Gilmer to have been a fair, honorable man who succeeded admirably in his other negotiations, but I cannot help thinking that he did not act in this affair of the Harwoods with his accustomed caution. He should not have made the young man come to the Isle of Wight and then put him off with an excuse that could not hold. He had engaged Bonnycastle within a week and that too without seeing him but once; he had absolute powers, and if he did not like young Harwood on personal acquaintance he should, I think, have found some other way of dismissing him than such an excuse. Besides if he had not liked the young man he should not have even hinted at his going to the United States at his own risk. But, I repeat, it is not well to judge too hastily in such matters. Gilmer was probably in a hurry to get back and had possibly been wearied by the elder Harwood's importunities. If one can judge by a letter, however, William Harwood was not the man to be treated so summarily. The Harwood letters it should be observed do not breathe a suspicion of any questionable treatment. I alone am responsible for these criticisms and they are the only ones I have to make on Mr. Gilmer's management of a tedious and difficult commission.[1]

I have so far said nothing about his purchases for the library; and now I can only mention that he bought most of the books from Bohn, and was much assisted by his banker, Mr. Marx.[2]

---

[1] John Harwood, Esq., M. D., F. R. S., &c., died at St. Leonards on the Sea, September 7th, 1854. I can find no obituary notice of him either in the Gentleman's Magazine or the Athenæum for this year.

A Wm. Harwood, M. D., was the author of a book on the "Curative influence of the Southern Coast of England," which was both praised and abused (G.'s M., 1828, Part 2, Supplement). I do not know whether this was our friend or not.

[2] Mr. Madison will hardly seem to some a fit person to apply to for a catalogue of theological books; but he did make out such a list for the University. See his writings, III, 450.

On the 5th day of October he sailed from Cowes in the packet Crisis, bound for New York.

Thus three quarters of a century after Bishop Berkeley had discouraged Dr. Johnson from trying to obtain English teachers for the new King's College in New York, Mr. Jefferson and Mr. Gilmer succeeded admirably in their trying and important task.[1]

.

---

[1] Berkeley's Works (Fraser), IV, 322. Letter from Berkeley to Johnson, Aug. 23d, 1749.

CHAPTER V.

CONCLUSION.

Thirty-five days after sailing from Cowes the packet Crisis arrived in New York. How Gilmer fared on the voyage will be seen from an almost too realistic letter written to Judge Carr on the 14th of November. This letter will be given presently. In the meantime on the 12th and 13th of the same month two letters were sent to Mr. Jefferson. In the first of these a list of the five professors was given and it was stated that they would arrive in ten days from the date of the letter. As will be seen later the hopes thus raised in Mr. Jefferson's breast were to be cruelly deferred. Gilmer also states that he could not hear of a single man in England fit for the chair of Natural History. In the second letter Campbell is said to have been the best friend Virginia had among all the writers of Great Britain. The letter also suggests John Torrey of West Point as the best person in America for the chair of Natural History. It may be mentioned here that President Monroe had some months since suggested Torrey and Percival, the poet and geologist, for chairs in the new University. We also find that Gilmer had been compelled to promise all the professors a fixed salary of $1,500 except Dr. Blaettermann, who, he thinks, should be placed on the same footing with the rest. I now give portions of the letter to Dabney Carr.

NEW YORK, *Nov.* 14, 1824.

Most dear Friend,

Having concluded all my arrangements in England much
to my satisfaction, I thought to return with triumph to the
light & bosom of my friends.   Fatal reverse of all my hopes !
here am I chained like Prometheus, after 35 days of anguish
at sea, such as man never endured.   I hold sea sickness
nothing, I laughed at it, as I went over—but to have added
to it a raging & devouring fever aggravated by want of
medicine, of food, of rest, of attendance, & the continued tossing
of the " rude imperious surge," form a combination of miseries
not easily imagined, & never before, I believe, exhibited.   I
am reduced to a shadow, and disordered throughout my whole
system.   My liver chiefly it is thought.   Among other symp-
toms, while I was in mid ocean, a horrible impostumation,
such as I supposed only accompanied the plague, in the form
of anthrax or carbuncle, appeared on my left side, low as I
was.   I neglected it till it was frightful—it required lancing
—but not a man could I get to do it—some were sea sick—
others indifferent, I called one who said he was a Doctor, &
desired him to cut it open—we had no lancet, no scalpel, no
knife that was fit, & finding him a timid booby, whose hand
shook, I took with my own hand a pair of scissors I happened
to have, and laid open my own flesh. . . . . . We had no
caustic, & I had to apply blue stone, which was nearly the
same sort of dressing, as the burning pitch to the bare nerves
of Ravaillac—yet I am no assassin—all the way I repeated,

"Sweet are the uses of adversity, &c."

I must turn this to some account—in this world I cannot,
but I " lay the flattering unction to my soul" that he who
suffers well never suffers in vain.   Such is the martyrdom I
have endured for the Old Dominion—she will never thank
me for it—but I will love & cherish her as if she did. . . . .

For over a month the poor fellow was confined at New
York, but he was not idle.   Mr. Jefferson answered his letters
on Nov. 21st, giving an account of the University buildings
and of his endeavors to get the books and baggage of the professors through without duty.   In a note of November 22nd
he implores Gilmer not to desert them by refusing the professorship of law—this being the only thing he has to complain
of in all his agent's conduct.

On the 29th of November John Torrey[1] wrote from West
Point declining the professorship of natural history on the
ground that he was well satisfied with his present position,
but recommending Dr. John Patton Emmet, of New York,
in these words: "His talents as chemist and scholar, and
standing as a gentleman are of the first rank.   I know him
well and know none before him."   This recommendation
brought about an interview between Dr. Emmet and Mr.
Gilmer, the result of which was the election of the former to
the chair which had given so much trouble.   Dr. Emmet was
a son of the Irish patriot and distinguished lawyer, Thomas
Addis Emmet.   Both father and son contributed to Gilmer's
comfort during his confinement, as did also John Randolph
of Roanoke, whom Gilmer had seen in England and who
passed through New York during the latter's sickness.   Gilmer's relations with this eccentric man were always of the
pleasantest kind—a circumstance somewhat remarkable.[2]

At this time the young man had fully determined not to
accept the law professorship as there seemed too much likeli-
hood that, if he did accept, his health would render the position
a practical sinecure; for he would have to have an assistant

---

[1] Torrey left West Point shortly after (1827) and became professor of
botany and chemistry in the College of Physicians and Surgeons.   He
wrote many valuable works on botany and deserves to be remembered as
having been the instructor of Asa Gray.

[2] Wm. Pope, the eccentric character before alluded to, once wrote Gilmer
that John Randolph had declared him "the most intelligent and best informed man of his age in Virginia" (letter of Nov. 2nd, 1825).

and he knew that the Visitors would never give him up after
his valuable services and the consequent injury to his constitution.   He therefore endeavored to sound as to the situation
that distinguished jurist, Chancellor Kent, who had accepted
a position in Columbia College, where he was to deliver the
lectures which subsequently formed the basis of his Commentaries.   The politics of the Chancellor were an objection,
but his reputation as a jurist would make him a desirable
acquisition.   The negotiation did not go far, however, and
Gilmer had to content himself with proposing the name of
Dr. Emmet to the Visitors, cordially endorsing all that Torrey
had said about him.

In the meantime Messrs. Long and Blaettermann arrived
at New York, and after calling upon Gilmer, hastened to
Richmond, proceeding from the latter place to the University,
where they found their pavilions in readiness.   It was also
ascertained that Key, Dunglison, and Bonnycastle would sail
in the Competitor direct to Norfolk.

By the 22nd of December we find Gilmer in Norfolk, staying with his friend Tazewell.   On the same day Mr. Jefferson
wrote two letters to Cabell in Richmond, from the first of
which I take this extract :

" Mr. Long, professor of ancient languages, is located in his
apartments at the University.   He drew, by lot, Pavilion No.
V.   He appears to be a most amiable man, of fine understanding, well qualified for his department, and acquiring
esteem as fast as he becomes known.   Indeed I have great
hopes that the whole selection will fulfill our wishes."

The second letter was of a more private nature and is given
almost entire :

MONTICELLO, *Dec.* 22, 1824.

Dear Sir,—Let the contents of this letter be known to you
and myself only.   We want a professor of Ethics.   Mr. Madison and myself think with predilection, of George Tucker,
our member of Congress.   You know him, however, better

than we do. Can we get a better? Will he serve? You
know the emoluments, and that the tenure is in fact for life,
the lodgings comfortable, the society select, &c. If you ap-
prove of him, you may venture to propose it to him, and ask
him if he will accept. I say "you may venture," because
three of us could then be counted on, and we should surely
get one, if not more, or all, of the other four gentlemen.[1] . . .

Mr. Cabell did sound Mr. Tucker, and after some delibera-
tions that gentleman consented to be a candidate for the chair
of ethics, to which position he was elected by the Visitors in
March, 1825. At the same time Dr. Emmet was elected to
the chair of natural history, and only the chair of law
remained unfilled. Of Mr. Tucker's acquirements much
might be said were not my space nearly exhausted. He had
already acquired a reputation as a good lawyer and a faithful
congressman, and had published some essays of value and
a novel. He subsequently did twenty years of excellent
work in his professorship, and greatly increased his reputation
as an author by his Life of Jefferson and his History of the
United States.

But my reader must not imagine that the Evil Genius
of Protection did not croak and flap its bat-like wings when
five British subjects were imported to ruin the mind of the
American youth; or, as the Boston *Gazette* put it, to disgust
them with anecdotes of "My Lord This" and "His Grace
That." No—the following choice specimens of the journal-
ism of the day will dispel any such comfortable idea—they
are taken from the Richmond *Enquirer* of December 11th,
1824:

"IMPORTATION OF PROFESSORS.

"[From the Boston *Courier.*]

"'The Richmond *Enquirer* informs the public, that Mr. Gilmer of that city who went to England in May to *procure profess-*

---

[1] Jefferson-Cabell Correspondence, pages 323, 324.

ors for the University of Virginia has returned and that he has been very successful in obtaining Professors, who were to sail from London in the Trident, about the 16th of October. On this the editor of the Connecticut *Journal* very properly remarks:

"'What American can read the above notice without indignation. Mr. Jefferson might as well have said that his *taverns* and *dormitories* should not be built with American bricks and have sent to Europe for them, as to import a group of Professors. We wish well to his College, but must think it a pity, that an agent should be dispatched to Europe for a suite of Professors. Mr. Gilmer could have fully discharged his mission, with half the trouble and expense, by a short trip to New England.'

"[From the Philadelphia *Gazette.*]

"'Or, we may be permitted to add, by a still shorter trip to Philadelphia. But because Pennsylvania does not produce Stump-Orators and Presidents, the Virginians conclude that it produces nothing else of value, forgetful that the first physicians, philosophers, historians, astronomers, and printers, known in American Annals have been citizens of our State. This sending of a Commission to Europe, to engage professors for a new University, is we think one of the greatest insults the American people have received.'

"We excuse the wit of our Boston and Philadelphia Editors, wishing them next time a better subject on which to employ it. It is by no means our desire to disparage the wise men of the East or the philosophers of Philadelphia, past, present or to come. We have had the misfortune, it is true, of producing two or three Presidents, and some fair stump orators (not to speak of Patrick Henry, R. H. Lee, John Randolph, or Littleton Waller Tazewell), but we do not see the mighty sin we commit either against good morals or good manners in looking out for the best Professors we can obtain for our rising University—nay of sending to G. Britain for Professors of the languages, mathematics and physics, if from any cause whatever it was not easy to obtain them in N. England or Pennsylvania. S. Carolina employs Dr. Cooper, has she been censured for her judicious selection? But no man can as well explain the motives of this visit as Mr. Jefferson himself, who in the ·

late report to the Legislature of Virginia has anticipated and answered, in the most appropriate manner, every exception that has been taken to the North. . . . ."[1]

I may remark that the case of Dr. Cooper does not at all apply, for he had been in this country nearly 30 years, and was not specially imported. In the same paper, however, I find an extract from the New York *American*, which represents a more liberal class of our population.

" We have heard with pleasure of the arrival of Messrs. Long and Blaettermann, the professors of ancient and modern languages in the University of Virginia. They are well known and highly esteemed in England. Their talents and acquirements will doubtless be highly advantageous to the cause of Public Instruction in the country. The other Professors of this Institution, Messrs. Key, Bonnycastle and Dunglison are daily expected."

In the meantime the Competitor had not put in an appearance, and great was the consternation on all sides. The newspapers gave accounts of terrific gales on the coast of England at the very time Key and his friends were to sail. Gilmer and Cabell were busy writing to Mr. Jefferson trying to allay the old gentleman's fear, but greatly alarmed themselves. Day after day passed and the date fixed upon for opening the University (February 1st) drew near. Lying stories were set in circulation and many predicted that the University would never succeed after all the delay. But on January 30th a gleam of hope came. Cabell had seen in a Norfolk paper that the Competitor was still in Plymouth on the 5th of December, and so had escaped the October gale. To his letter announcing this fact Jefferson made the following reply which is interesting enough to quote.

---

[1] If the New England editors had known that two of the first professorships had been offered to Bowditch and Ticknor, their language would probably have been milder; and what are we to think of the application of Rufus King to Mr. Drury?

8

MONTICELLO, *February* 3, 1825.

Dear Sir,—Although our professors were on the 5th of December still in an English port, that they were safe raises me from the dead; for I was almost ready to give up the ship. That was eight weeks ago, and they may therefore be daily expected.

In most public seminaries, text books are prescribed to each of the several schools, as the *norma docendi* in that school; and this is generally done by authority of the trustees. I should not propose this generally in our University, because, I believe none of us are so much at the heights of science in the several branches as to undertake this, and therefore that it will be better left to the professors, until occasion of inter-ference shall be given. But there is one branch in which we are the best judges, in which heresies may be taught, of so interesting a character to our own State, and to the United States, as to make it a duty in us to lay down the principles which shall be taught. It is that of government. Mr. Gilmer being withdrawn, we know not who his successor may be. He may be a Richmond lawyer, or one of that school of quondam federalism, now consolidation. It is our duty to guard against the dissemination of such principles among our youth, and the diffusion of that poison, by a previous prescrip-tion of the texts to be followed in their discourses. . . . .[1]

These books were actually chosen by Jefferson and Madison as we learn from a letter of the latter's dated February 8th, 1825 (Writings, III, 481); but, although it would seem that the progressive statesman had receded from his own excellent doctrine that the present generation should not hamper pos-terity, and although a greater than the Andover Controversy would seem to be here in germ, when we read the list of texts prescribed our apprehensions are abated. They consisted of

---

[1] Jefferson-Cabell Correspondence, page 339.

311]   *English Culture in Virginia.*   123

(1) The Declaration of Independence, (2) The Federalist, (3) The Virginia Resolutions of '98 against the Alien and Sedition Laws " which appeared to accord with the predominating sense of the people of the United States"; and (4) The Inaugural Speech and Farewell Address of President Washington " as conveying political lessons of peculiar value."

On the same day that this letter was written Cabell wrote that as Gilmer had three times declined the law chair, it might be offered advantageously to Chancellor Tucker of Winchester. He also proposed a very impracticable scheme which I was surprised at so sensible a man's making, viz., to attach to the professorship a small chancery district consisting of Albemarle and four contiguous counties.[1]   Negotiations were accordingly opened with Tucker but in vain.   He was destined, however, to fill the chair from 1840 .to 1844.

In the meantime the long wished for " Competitor " arrived at Norfolk and on Thursday evening, February 10th, Key wrote the welcome intelligence to Gilmer, who lost no time in informing Mr. Jefferson.   Key and his companions passed through Richmond and attracted the most favorable notice. The battle had been won, even the capital city of the enemy had been completely disarmed.

On the seventh day of March, 1825, the University of Virginia was formally opened with the five foreign professors and forty students.   Professors Tucker and Emmet arrived shortly after, and students kept coming in until on September 30th they numbered 116.   The first term closed on December 15th, 1825.   The professorship of law had in the meantime, after having been refused by Mr. P. P. Barbour and Judge Carr, been offered to Judge Wm. A. C. Dade, of the general court.   Judge Dade seems to have been a fine lawyer and a man of some classical attainments; but the situation did not charm him.   Accordingly Mr. Jefferson fell back upon his first choice and wrote him an urgent letter.   Gilmer's health now

---

[1] Same, page 338.

seemed sufficiently restored to enable him to undertake the
work, and as he felt that the strain of public life would
not suit him in the future, he answered Mr. Jefferson's
more than flattering appeal by accepting the position. The
visitors, therefore, unanimously elected him and he looked
forward to delivering his first lecture at the beginning of the
second term. But fate decided it otherwise, his health again
broke down and he realized that this time he was disabled
forever.

Then the visitors turned to Wirt, who had been thought
of long before, but whose high position under the government
had seemed to preclude all chance of his acceptance. To
make the offer more attractive, it was resolved to create a
new office of "President of the University of Virginia" which
should be held by Mr. Wirt, but, if he declined, should not
go into effect. This was in April, 1826. Wirt preferred to
settle in Baltimore and so the ill-fated chair was offered to
John Taylor Lomax—a lawyer of some distinction, residing
near Fredericksburg. Mr. Lomax accepted and Mr. Jefferson's agony was at last over. On the 21st of April he wrote
to Cabell that Lomax had paid them a visit and charmed
them all.[1]

It would seem at first thought that my work is now accomplished and that that agreeable word "finis" is all that
remains to be written. But we have not yet taken leave of
the man whose labor this study was written to commemorate;
and a few words as to the fortunes of those whom he brought
over, would not appear amiss.

And now briefly of the latter point.[2]

Mr. Key finding that the climate of Virginia did not agree

[1] Jefferson-Cabell Correspondence, page 377.
[2] My chapters in Dr. Adams' work, before referred to, are a proper supplement to this study, and to them the reader is referred. Volumes III
and IV of Madison's Writings are the best original source I know of for
the period from 1826–36.

with him was compelled to resign in 1827 and to return to England.   There his high abilities were recognized by a position in the newly established University of London, and we marvel at the versatility of the man when we find that the remainder of his long and useful life was devoted to philology.   He died in 1875, and his recently published Latin dictionary is the latest monument to his labor.

On Mr. Key's resignation, Mr. Bonnycastle was transferred to the chair of mathematics.   This gentleman at first had some trouble as to a bond which he was under to the British government, and which was forfeited by his coming to America.   A slight misunderstanding arose between Gilmer and himself owing to this fact and to the hasty drawing up of the contract between them.   But mutual explanations happily settled the matter.   Mr. Bonnycastle held the chair of mathematics until his death in 1840, and was, I believe, the first in this country to introduce the use of the ratio method of the trigonometrical functions.

Mr. Long received a call to the London University in 1828, but he left a worthy representative behind him.   In my chapter in Dr. Adams' work, I give a sketch of the work of Dr. Gessner Harrison, whom Long nominated as his successor. That sketch, taken mainly from an address by the Rev. John A. Broadus, cannot be repeated here.   It is sufficient to say that Long kept Dr. Harrison posted on all the latest German discoveries in philology, and that the students of the University of Virginia were familiar with the labors of Bopp before that great man was fully recognized in Germany itself.   Of Mr. Long's subsequent labors for English education, I surely need not speak.

With respect to Dr. Blaettermann, I have been singularly unfortunate in collecting information.   The few notices I have seen of him, speak highly of his attainments, but are not so pleasant in other respects.   Gilmer seems to have seen what he calls a "puff" about him in one of the English papers, and Dr. Gessner Harrison wrote in a kindly way of him in Duyckinck's Cyclopaedia.[1]

Dr. Robley Dunglison's name is so well known in this country that I need only say that he remained eight years at the University, and laid the foundation of what has proved to be a remarkably successful medical school. Mr. Jefferson, in his last illness, trusted entirely to his skill. His work in medical literature is known even to general readers. The subsequent careers of the native professors are foreign to my purpose, and it only remains for us to take our leave of the man we have learnt to know so well, Francis Walker Gilmer.

The tale is soon told; and being sad, this is surely best. After returning from New York, he was thrown back by the carelessness of a servant, who left a window open by his bed all night. As he was naturally delicate, his health was rapidly undermined. He could attend to little business, and left Richmond for Albemarle, from whence he went to one of the Virginia Springs. The little business he could attend to was of a painful nature, being connected with the ruined fortunes of his old friend, ex-governor Thomas Mann Randolph. The trip to the Springs buoyed him up, and he accepted the law professorship, as we have seen. But his disorders becoming worse, he was compelled to resign, and after a lingering illness of many weeks, he died at the residence of one of his relatives in Albemarle, on the 25th of February, 1826. One of his last acts was to leave a sum of money for the purchase of a communion service for the Episcopal Church in Charlottesville. He passed away in the arms of his brother Peachy, who has recorded in the volume before me that " he died in the faith of Jesus Christ." Upon the last letter which he received from his dear friend, Wm. Wirt, Gilmer wrote these few lines in pencil—the last writing he ever did: " Dear & beloved Mr. W.—Nothing but a last

[1] Dr. Adams cites an article in the Southern Literary Messenger for January, 1842, which throws light on the characters of the early professors.

hope could have induced me to take such a liberty with you.[1] I have scarcely any hope of recovering & was but a day or two ago leaving you my last souvenir. I have not written to you because I love & admire you & am too low to use my own hand with convenience. Farewell to you & to all a family I have esteemed so well."

I promised to give a detailed account of Mr. Gilmer's literary work, but I now find that from want of space I cannot keep that promise. Perhaps it is as well that I should not; the world has forgotten what he wrote—I would fain hope that it will not forget what he did. There are MS. essays extant on "The causes of the ascent of vapour" and "Certain phenomena of vision," which it will be best to leave undisturbed, although they certainly show an original and inquiring mind. In the *Analectic Magazine* for July, 1818, will be found an interesting account of a visit paid to the Cherokees in Tennessee, probably in company with Mr. Corrèa, but the modern reader would be apt to think that the article dealt more with the Greeks and Romans than was necessary. The essay on the Natural Bridge, which was translated by Pictet, appeared, I believe, in the XVth volume of the same magazine. This I have not seen. In January, 1828, Fielding Lucas, Jun., of Baltimore, issued a small volume of "Sketches, Essays and Translations, by the late Francis Walker Gilmer, of Virginia," Mr. Wirt contributing a preface. This contained the revised "Sketches of American Orators," by far, it seems to me, his best performance, and containing some good criticism, "A vindication of the laws limiting the rate of interest on loans," an answer to Bentham, which, though it shows a great deal of legal learning, inclines too much to reasoning by analogy, and hardly settles the matter; and certain translations from the French economists lent him by Du Pont de Nemours. These, with the volume of

---

[1] That is—using Wirt's own letter for his reply.

reports previously mentioned, constitute all of Gilmer's writings with which I am acquainted.[1]

His learning was certainly curious and enormous. He seems to have been a fine lawyer, perhaps the most learned of his day in Virginia; it can hardly be said that he was a philosophic jurist. He was also a good classical scholar and botanist—something of a philologian and physical experimenter—and personally one of the most agreeable of companions. There are many things in these letters which show a delicate wit and some of the turns of his mind are as original as they are entertaining. This may serve as a sample. Speaking of Wirt's success he says that he has heard that Wirt created as much astonishment in Washington as the Duke of Buckingham did in Madrid, "there having been no such comet in that hemisphere."[2]

How Mr. Gilmer was regarded by his contemporaries may be seen from the following letter:

WASHINGTON, *Dec.* 27, 1827.

My dear Sir,

I am extremely sensible to your kind attention & highly obliged by it. Everything connected with my late friend, your dear brother, is dear to me. I am now probably as near my journey's end as he was on his return from that ill fated voyage to England, from which I date the disease that so

---

[1] I have seen it stated that he wrote some of the numbers of the "Old Bachelor," and several articles in the Virginia Evangelical and Literary Magazine, of which his friend, Dr. Rice, was editor. Both of these statements are probably true; but no mention is made of the matter in the Gilmer letters; nor is he stated to have been a contributor in the obituary notice of him in the ninth volume of the aforesaid magazine.

[2] I also find a characteristic sentence *à propos* of the strained relations between Wirt and Pinckney (relations more strained than Mr. Kennedy's tender heart would allow him to tell us). "You may never again have a chance of shivering his spear, which is not of mountain ash like that of Achilles, but, as Randolph said of his own, rather of the tobacco stick order, though pointed up like a small sword."

cruelly robbed us of him.   Whether we shall be permitted
to recognize our friends in a future world is beyond our ken
—but the belief is so consonant with the goodness of our
Creator & so consolatory to the heart of man that I would
fain indulge in it.

Accept, my dear Sir, my best wishes and respects—

Your obliged

To   J. R. of ROANOKE.

PEACHY R. GILMER ESQ.   .

Both Mr. Randolph and Mr. Wirt were applied to for an
epitaph; but neither felt equal to the task.   The letters from
which the foregoing was taken and which have been the basis
of this study were collected by Mr. Peachy Gilmer in 1833
and bound in two large volumes for the use of his descend-
ants.   Mr. Wirt was very loth to part with Gilmer's letter
to him, reserving at the last the letter written from Shakespeare's house and the leaf of Kenilworth ivy which accompanied it.

Francis Walker Gilmer, Virginia's benefactor, lies buried
at his old family seat, Pen Park, in Albemarle County.   Over
his remains is a plain stone recording the dates of his birth
and death and preserving the following epitaph, written by
himself, and almost as sad as Swift's—

> "Pray, stranger, allow one who never had peace while he lived,
> The sad Immunities of the Grave,
> *Silence* and *Repose.*"

ERRATUM.

For "*gigomaniac*" on page 9 read *gig-maniac*.   The quotation marks are
dropped because the writer is doubtful whether Carlyle ever used the
word—"*gigmanity*," which occurs in the essay on Boswell's Life, probably
occasioned the misapprehension.   But reviewing his work, after the lapse
of nearly a year, the writer finds himself wondering how Carlyle and so
many extraneous subjects got mixed up with what he intended to make the
simple record of a good man's life.

APPENDIX..

It seems well to preserve here three of the letters which Gilmer received from George Ticknor. In a few respects they appear to supplement those, relating to the same period, which have already delighted the world in that charming book—"The Life and Letters of George Ticknor." Good letters are too rare to be carelessly put aside, and I feel convinced that my readers will thank me for acting upon this conviction and presenting these.

I.

Göttingen King˟ of Hanover.
May 31st, 1816.

I am rejoiced to find my Dear Gilmer by the letter you sent by Mr. Terrell[1] that you have not forgotten me, though you have not heard from me. That this has been the case, however is no fault of mine. Immediately after receiving your letter of last May, I wrote to America to know where I should address to you, and since then I have made the same inquiry of Mr. Jefferson and in Paris but could learn nothing of you, until day before yesterday, when your very welcome letter came to tell me all I hoped to hear except that you had renounced your intention of coming to Europe. In this respect you have changed your plans; and as you intend to be a lawyer, I rather think you have done wisely. I too

---

[1] The young Virginian previously referred to.

have changed my plans, I have renounced the law altogether,
and determined to prolong my stay in Europe, that I may
do something towards making myself a scholar, and perhaps
you will smile, when I add that my determining motive to
this decision, of which I have long thought, was the admirable
means and facilities and inducements to study offered by a
German University. But however you may smile on the
other side of the Atlantic, you would if you were on this, do
just as I have done. My inclination is entirely & exclusively
to literature—the only question with me, therefore, was, where
I could best fit myself to pursue *haud passibus aequis* its
future progress & improvement. In England I found that
the vigorous spirit of youth was already fled though to be
sure in its place I found a green and honourable old age—in
France—where literature, its progress & success was always
much more intimately connected with the court than it ever
was in any other age or country if Rome under Augustus be
excepted,—in France it has long been the sport of political
revolutions & seems at last to be buried amidst the ruins of
national independence—and in the S(outh) of Europe, in
Portugal, Spain, and Italy centuries have passed over its
grave.—In Germany, however, where the spirit of letters first
began to be felt a little more than half a century ago, all is
still new & young, and the workings of this untried spirit
starting forth in fresh strength, & with all the advantages
which the labour and experience of other nations can give it
are truly astonishing. In America, indeed, we have but little
of these things, for our knowledge of all Europe is either
derived from the French, whose totally different manners, &
language & character prevents them from even conceiving
those of Germany, or from England, whose ancient prejudices
against every thing continental as yet prevent them from
receiving as it deserves a kindred literature. Still, however,
the English scholars have found out that the Germans are far
before them in the knowledge of antiquity, so that if you
look into an English Treatise on Bibliography you will find

nine tenths of the best editions of the classics to be German;
—and Mad. de Stael has told the world, tho' to be sure, very
imperfectly and unworthily, what a genial & original literature has sprung up in Germany within the last 50 years like
a volcano from the wastes & depths of the ocean.—But it is
not what they have already done, or what they are .at this
moment doing, astonishing as both are, which makes me hope
so much from these Germans. It is the free, & philosphical
spirit with which they do it—the contempt of all ancient
forms considered as such, and the exemption from all preju-
dice—above all, the unwearied activity with which they push·
forward, and the high objects they propose to themselves—it
is this, that makes me feel sure, Germany is soon to leave all
the rest of the world *very* far behind in the course of improvement—and it was this that determined me to remain here
rather than to pursue my studies in countries where this high
spirit has faded away.—

You may perhaps smile at all this, my dear Gilmer, and
think that my reasons for spending above a year and a half
in Göttingen are as bad as the revolution itself. If we live
twenty years, however, & then meet one another, you will be
prepared to tell me I have done right, for though the political
machine may at last grind Germany to powder, yet I am
satisfied that the spirit which was not extinguished or even
repressed by the French Usurpation will not be stopped in its
career by any revolution that is likely to happen before that
time, and in twenty years German literature, & science, and
learning will stand higher than those of any other modern
nation. Mr. Terrel, of course, I have not yet seen, but in a
little more than a year I shall, I suppose, find him in Germany; & if I can there do him any service, you may be
certain, that I shall not be found unfaithful to the remembrance of the many pleasant hours passed with you & owed
to you in Philadelphia and Washington. Farewell. I will
write to you soon again & you must write soon to me. Send
your letters to *Boston* care of E. Ticknor & they will certainly

reach me. Where is Winchester? Tell me all about it & about your situation. If it is near Monticello, remember me when you are there, & tell Mr. Jefferson that my only regret in determining to stay here is that I cannot have the pleasure of purchasing his books in Paris. I hope, however, as I have told him, still to find some way of being useful to him in Europe.

Yrs truly, GEORGE TICKNOR.

FRANCIS W. GILMER, ESQ.,
   Winchester, Virg.
Care of JOHN VAUGHAN, ESQ.,
   Philadelphia.

II.

GÖTTINGEN Jan. 30. 1817.

Your very welcome letter of Oct. 11. 1816. my dear Gilmer reached me a few days since and I thank you for it a thousand times.—It afforded me pleasure in every part except that in which you speak of your feeble health. My dear Gilmer, take care of yourself. I say this from an experience, which makes my warning solemn, and which should make it efficient.—One of the very first things that struck me on coming to Europe was, that their men of letters & professions here live much longer and enjoy lively & active faculties much later than in America.[1] And what is the reason? Not because our students labour harder—not because they exercise less—not because they smoke more or for any other of the twenty frivolous reasons that are given by anxious friends among us, for these are all disproved by the *fact* here, that a man of letters works from 12 to 16 hours a day—

---

[1] Here he adds on the side of the page—I have reduced this to an arithmetical fact by calculating the length of the lives of men of letters in Eng.(land) France, Spain, Italy, & Germany.

exercises not at all—smokes three fourths of his time &c &c.
—The reason is, that every man must have habits suited to
his occupations, whereas our men of letters are so few that
they are obliged to adopt the habits of persons about them
whose occupations are utterly different.   Thus we get up late
in the morning because breakfast is not to be had early with
convenience to the family—we dine late because our dinner
hour must conform to that of men of business—we give the
evening to the world because it is the fashion—and thus
having passed the whole day under the constraint of others,
we steal half the solitude & silence of the night to repair our
loss.   Under the influence of such habits our men of letters
in America seldom attain their fortieth year & often fall vic-
tims in the very threshold of active life.   The great faults
lie in the distribution of time and of meals.—A student should
certainly rise early, not only because Sir John Sinclair's Tables
show that early risers are always (*caeteris paribus*) the longest
livers but because anyone who has made the experiment will
tell you that the morning is the best time for labour.   It has
the advantages of silence & solitude for which we use the
evening and the *great* additional ones that mind & body are
then refreshed & quickened for exertion.   In the nature of
things therefore, the heaviest studies, whatever they may be,
should be the first in the day, & as far as it is possible, I
would have their weight diminished in each portion of time
until they cease, because by the fatigue of exercise, the faculties
become continually less capable of easy & dexterous exertion
without being compelled to it by excitement which afterwards
produces languor.   Then as to meals—I would not eat a
hearty American breakfast on first rising, for that is the very
time, when as the body is already strengthened & restored by
sleep, it needs least of all the excitement of hearty food.
Still less is the intrusion of craving hunger to be desired.—
For the first seven or eight hours, after rising therefore, I
have observed it best to keep the appetite merely still by
eating perhaps twice some very light food—bread & butter &

a cup of coffee &c—By that time the strength needs assistance
& the principal meal in the day should be made, which with
light food once or at most twice afterwards is sufficient until
" Nature's grand restorer" comes to fit mind & body for new
exertions. Observe, I pray you, that the two last hours in
the day should not as with us, be the hours chosen for the
severest labour, but should as much as possible, be hours of
very light reading, or absolute amusement & idleness for two
reasons, because the mind & body are then weary whether we
permit ourselves to feel it or not and because the excitement
of hard study just before going to bed prevents us from
enjoying "the sweet, the innocent sleep" which is so indispensable to refresh the faculties.—Now, my dear Gilmer, do
not say all this is theory & whim, for I know it—I *feel* it to
be fact. In America my health faded under eight, nine &
ten hours study in a day and I have lived in Göttingen a
year &· an half and grown stronger on studying more than
twelve hours a day. I rise at five o'clock in the morning
and my servant brings me immediately a cup of coffee & a
piece of bread—at IX I eat some bread and butter—at I I
dine—between VII & VIII in the evening I take some light
supper & at X go faithfully to bed & sleep the sleep that
knows no waking.—I do not beg you to do the same, for I
know not how much your health is reduced; but when you
have applied the needful means and restored yourself to your
usual strength—*then* I do beseech you to adopt this or some
other system equally simple, strict and rational and do not
fear the result.—I speak on this subject with an earnestness
uncommon to me, for I have more than common reasons.—
I have lost many friends though I am still young—some
whose talents and acquirements would, in riper years, have
given a new character to letters among us, and now that I live
in the midst of men who have grown old under labour which
always seemed to me without the limits of human strength
and have compared the annals of literature in other countries
with its condition here, I can look back and see how gradually

and surely the health and lives of nearly every one of these
friends were destroyed by their conformity to the habits of
the society in which they lived—by the inversion of their day
in study and in meals—& in short, by attempting to live at
once like students & like men whose occupations are anything
but intellectual—Beware, then, of this, my dear Gilmer—The
world expects a great deal from your talents and you can
easily fulfill these expectations, if you will but preserve your
health by accomodating your habits to the nature of your
occupations.

When I began, I am sure, I intended to have said but a
word on this subject.—You will not, however, mistake my
reason. If I valued your health less, I should be less anxious
to have you preserve it & if I had not placed a portion of my
happiness on the continuance of your life & did not know that
you are one who can fill so much of the chasm in our intellectual state, I should not have been betrayed beyond a letter's
limit on a subject which after all hardly comes within the
rubricks of correspondence.

You inquire after works on Jurisprudence and on Political
Economy.—On the last there is very little in German Authors
& what there is of good, is founded on Adam Smith & Burke.
This is the consequence of their miserable political situation,
divided into little independent Principalities, which makes all
their political interests little & insignificant & thus prevents
liberal general discussions on great interests & questions.—
On Jurisprudence they have books to confusion & satiety;
but few, I apprehend, that would much interest an American
Lawyer, however extensive he makes his horizon, unless it be
good histories & commentaries on the Roman Law, in which,
however, the present state of its practice in Germany is, again,
the chief point kept in view.—If you would like any of these
(the best are in German not Latin) I can procure them for
you through a friend who will pass the next summer here,
though I shall not myself—while at the same time, if you
should like anything from France or Italy I will gladly serve

you in person as I shall divide the year that begins in May between them. Command me I pray you without reserve, for besides the pleasure I should feel in serving you, I feel a gratification always in sending home good books, for I know I can in no way so directly & efficiently serve the interests of letters in my native country.

When you write to Monticello or visit there, I pray you that I may be remembered, for out of my own home I know not where I have passed a few days so pleasantly.—Remember me, too, yourself—write to me often directing your letters as before care of E. Tinckor Boston—& in your next tell me your health is better, if you would tell me what will most please me.—Yrs truly GEO. TICKNOR.

Addressed

FRANCIS W. GILMER, ESQ.,
            Winchester (*Virg.*)
Care of
        JOHN VAUGHAN ESQ.
                    Philadelphia.

Endorsed—Forwarded by J. V. who having no letter himself wishes to learn something of the traveller.
PHIL. *April* 26ᵗʰ 1817

III.

ROME *Nov.* 25. 1817.

Your letter of May 2d., my dear Gilmer, reached me in Paris three months ago, since which I have, until lately, been in such constant movement that I have been able to write to nobody except to my own family. I thank you for it, however, with a gratitude as warm as if I had been able to answer it the same week I received it, and pray you no less earnestly to continue me the favor of your correspondence than if I had been able to do more to merit it. What grieves me the most, however, is the affair of your Books. You desire me to procure for you several works on law, literature &c but desire me first to consult with Mr. Terrel to know whether he had not already purchased them. This letter I

received only six days before I was obliged to leave Paris,
and, of course, all consultation with him was impossible. I,
however, did the next best thing, it seemed to me, I could,—
I took the letter to Geneva—added to Mr. Terrel's list the
books I did not find on it, for, on inquiry, I learned he, too,
had been able to do nothing,—and gave him the address of
the De Bures Booksellers, who, as they have twice sent Books
to Mr. Jefferson & often to other Persons in America, will no
doubt be able to send yours safely. Indeed, I trust, they
have by this time reached you; and this is my only consola-
tion when I think of them; for nothing gives me so much
pleasure as to do precisely this sort of service to my friends;
because I know how delightful and difficult it is for them to
receive good books from Europe and how much more useful
a service I render to my country by sending such than I
can ever render in any other way. You will have your books
I doubt not, but I should rather you would have had them
through me.—   .

In Geneva, I saw a good deal of Mr. Terrel. I wish, we
had a great many more young men like him in Europe,—for
he is improving his time, I am persuaded, remarkably well,
instead of losing it and worse than losing it, as ninety nine
out of the hundred who come here, do. He is destined, I
presume, by the course of studies he talked to me about, to be
a Politician and though that is a kind of trade for which I
have little respect in any country, I am glad he seems to be
learning its elements with such enlarged & philosophical
views; and especially that he mingles with it no small por-
tions of physical science & literature. The old adage may be
true in Europe respecting learning,—that it is better to cultivate a Province than to conquer an Empire—but really for an
American politician and for any one engaged in the liberal
administration of a free government, a little of that equivocal
information that we call General Knowledge is absolutely
indispensable and will prevent him from doing and saying
a thousand of the foolish things our Politicians do & say

so often. Terrel, however, pursues his studies, as the professors told me[,] in such a manner, that all his important
knowledge will really be thorough and, what it. gave me no
less pleasure to remark, he has so lived among the persons,
with whom he has been intimately connected at Geneva, as to
gain not only their respect but their affection, and confidence.

Since leaving Geneva two months ago, my whole journey
has been mere Poetry; and I have truly enjoyed myself more
in this short space than in all the time that preceded it, since
I left home. The Plains of Lombardy are the Garden of
Europe and the world. When this phrase is applied elsewhere,
I know very well how to interpret it and what qualifications
are to be made; but when I recollect the waste of fertility
formed by the bed of the Po & its tributary waters—the
bright verdue of the fields—the luxuriant abundance of the
harvests—the several parcels of land marked by, fanciful
copses of trees—& the whole united by the graceful festoons
of the vines, hanging with purple & heavy with the wealth
of autumn—while everywhere about me were the frolicks and
gaiety of the vintage, it seems to me as if I had been in fairy
land or amidst the unmingled beauties of the primitive cre-
ation,

> "for nature here
> Wantoned as in her prime, and played at will
> Her virgin fancies, pouring forth more sweet
> Wild above rule or art, .enormous bliss.[1]

And then, too, as soon as as you have passed the Apennines,
you come upon the very classical soil of Roman literature and
history and every step you take is marked by some monument
that bears witness to their glories. This continues until you
arrive, twenty five miles before you reach Rome, at the last
village and enter upon the unalleviated desolation of the Cam-
pagna. I cannot express to you the secret horror I felt while
passing over this mysterious waste, which tells such a long

---

[1] Here a strange hand has inserted P. Le. B. V. v. 294.

tale to the feelings and the imagination or how glad I felt, as
if I had awaked from a dreadful dream, when turning sud-
denly round a projecting height of Monte Mario, at whose
feet the Tiber winds in sullen majesty along, Rome with its
seven hills and all its towers & turrets & Pinnacles—with the
castle of St. Angelo and the Dome of St. Peters—Rome in all
the solemnity & splendor of the Eternal City burst at once
upon my view—But, my dear G——, if I begin thus to tell
you of all my (?) in my travel's history, I shall never stop.

Farewell, then; and remember me always and write to me
often.—Remember me to Mr. Jefferson with great respect,
when you see him or write to him and believe me yours very
sincerely

GEO. TICKNOR.

My address remains always the same—E. Ticknor, Boston.—

www.ingramcontent.com/pod-product-compliance
Lightning Source LLC
Chambersburg PA
CBHW030605270326
41927CB00007B/1057